THE
SUPREME
BEING

THE
SUPREME
BEING

Birinder Bhullar

Outskirts Press, Inc.
Denver, Colorado

Contents

Introduction

Life exists within a limitless unknown. No mind has ever been able to fathom or control the Infinite Power behind Creation. The Self who has not experienced the Supreme Being does not know its reality. Such a Self exists in a world of illusion. Power, beauty, money, and possessions fascinate it, and keep it inebriated. Death, disease, and disaster are the only times it awakens. Only during these moments does it feel the insignificance and vulnerability of purely material living. If there were no pain, misery, fear, or loneliness, the Self would never have sought beyond the reality of the mind. Life is too short and invaluable to be wasted. It is meant to be a search for the Ultimate Reality. The real treasure to be found in life is awakening to The Truth. It is the only thing that is eternal; which even death cannot take away from the Self. Experiencing the Supreme Being is a reunion with The Source. It is a homecoming. It is the ultimate freedom. Only a life lived toward it can have true meaning, joy, and peace.

Experiencing the Supreme Reality is the core desire of the Self. It is the original urge which caused Creation. The

Self has lived many lives in separation from the Supreme Being. Deep within, the Self remembers the love, bliss, and peace of the original oneness. The Self's deepest pangs are for reunion with the Supreme Source. Revelation of The Truth will awaken the Self to its Reality.

The Supreme Being is expressing itself in everything in Creation. From the smallest particle to the entire Universe -- everything is its expression. Creation arose out of love: love to experience; love to know the ultimate. The Supreme Consciousness wished to experience itself. A spark of this original desire is hidden deep within every heart. It has to become a flame. The quest to experience the Supreme Reality has to become conscious. The Self has to feel this quest within its heart.

The Self loves itself. It seeks the power to realize all desires of its heart. It wishes to live forever. It wishes to become completely secure. This cannot happen till the Self experiences the Supreme Being. The Self prays to the Supreme Being to realize wishes beyond its power, and to feel protected from the unknown. But it does not seek to experience the Supreme Being and know The Truth. All wishes of the Self will be fulfilled, once the Self experiences True Reality. What greater empowerment could there be than awakening to your true relationship with the Supreme Being? What greater knowing than coming to know the ultimate reality of your own Self and the entirety of Creation?

While the Self lives without relating with the Supreme Being, inner unrest, turmoil, and uncertainty will not end. There is endless suffering within the Reality of the mind. There are many illusions in it, and it is incomplete -- in it, fear controls life. The Self is compelled to seek more and more power in order to feel secure. It never seems enough. The Self never feels free from all that is unpleasant and can harm. Nothing within this Reality can give peace, clarity, and security. Nothing within it can unburden the Self.

The Supreme Being is the true reality of the Self. It is the only Reality. It is the true destination of the Self. Seeking it is the purpose of life. Begin living to become one with it. Why wait till meaningless and unnatural living makes life completely unbearable? Life is not a punishment. It is meant to be an awakening: an experience of love, a blissful experience of Reality. Experiencing oneness with the Supreme Being liberates the Self, and gives it a life of Love, Faith, Fearlessness, Peace, and Happiness. The other shore of such a life is absolute union with the Supreme Consciousness.

The Supreme Being is infinite. The Supreme Truth is suprarational. It is inexpressible as a whole through the mind. It is beyond the grasp of the mind. It is beyond the reach of both interpreted religion and science. The Self can experience it only by becoming one. To become one, the mind has to dissolve. It is the barrier.

You do not know enough about the Supreme Being. If you believe already, you must desire to know more, and seek to experience it. Belief in and of itself will not help. If you disbelieve, know more first -- how can you deny a thing you know little about? Belief or disbelief can become a reality only through experience. Anything that has not been experienced will remain a belief, in which doubt can never end. Revealed Truth will put the Self on the path, but doubt will not dissolve till the Supreme Being is experienced.

The mind maintains the illusion of separation between the Self and the Supreme Being. The mind is the Self's past. The mind by its inherent nature is past-dependent, relative, and doubting. The mind was required originally to separate and mature the individuality of the Self, but has to dissolve once the individuality has crystallized -- otherwise, oneness with the Supreme Being cannot be experienced.

The path toward the Supreme Being requires complete surrender. It requires a lot of persistence and hard work. An immense depth of Love and Faith is required in a seeker, to endlessly seek for an experience. Every area of life has to become a seeking for the Ultimate Reality. It requires total surrender to Creation and to life, as well.

The Supreme Being can be experienced only in the present life on Earth. It cannot be postponed to any afterlife. If the Self does not experience the Supreme Being here, it will not find it in any other world or realm. Another life would have to be lived to complete the search for The Truth.

It does not matter whether you are a theist, atheist, agnostic, or have some other belief -- the Self still seeks answers to many questions: Who am I? Why am I here? What is the mind? What is life? What is peace? What is happiness? What do I really want? What is my eternal home? How did I forget about it? What is my bondage? What is ultimate freedom? What is my fear? What is my insecurity? What is completeness? What is True Living? This book will share the answers to these questions and many more, from experiences with the Supreme Reality.

The Supreme Reality includes everything. Experiencing it will answer all questions, forever. Do not waste life debating and conflicted about True Reality, basing your perceptions on partial knowledge and past conditioning of the mind. Experience the Supreme Reality, at least once, and then decide.

You cannot have a real experience of the Supreme Being, nor can you experience ultimate Self-Knowing, with a shallow knowledge of The Truth, with on-and-off seeking;

you cannot have these real experiences with one or two changes in your life, or with knowledge of the Supreme Being just from reading books. You cannot have real experience by debating one book after reading another, or by attempting to synthesize knowledge gathered from many different sources. However, these things are good, in the very early stages, as preparation for a deeper seeking. Eventually, being near a Master is an entirely different experience. Be near a Master and you will know the difference between just knowing about, and seeking to experience. A Master is living The Truth. A Master has to say very little. A Master never concludes The Truth. The shallower The Truth, the more the mind can understand it and conclude it.

Religious scriptures are the truest and richest source of information about the Ultimate Truth. But these great books have infinite dimensions, and are open-ended, like The Truth. They are living expressions, to point toward the Truth, and no ultimate conclusions can be drawn about their meaning. You cannot read and know the meaning of their content like ordinary books. Their meanings have infinite dimensions, have to be evolved with time, and have to be uniquely interpreted for guiding every Self on the path. Before experiencing The Truth, these vast dimensions cannot be seen. Devotion and belief in them is essential to mature a seeker. Finally, only actual experience of the Supreme Being can reveal what The Truth is.

When you experience The Truth, you will know that religion and science are both parts of it, and there is no conflict. In fact, without being both religious and scientific on the path, you can never experience the Supreme Reality. All true Mystics used both. Both depend upon faith as the basis for a search into the unknown. In the scientific domain faith is called axioms and assumptions; in the religious domain it is called beliefs and faith. But both require proof

-- only experience can give it. Beyond experiencing reality, science and religion do not remain separate.

A block to experiencing the Supreme Being is that the Self is ashamed to accept a personal relationship with it in public. It fears it will be seen as irrational. Times are changing, though. Unless you find the courage to be completely honest about your love and seeking for the Supreme Being, an experience will never happen.

There is a way to live for people on the path. Life has several spheres: Self, Family, Society, Creation, and God. You have to answer all of them. This is the only kind of life that can be called complete, and which prepares the Self for the experience. Every Prophet, Saint, and Mystic highly emphasized it for arriving at The Truth.

When the Self experiences the Supreme Being, a wonderful metamorphosis of its reality happens. The quest of many lives ends.
It is like the coming of spring and bloom. The truth is revealed. The heart and feelings revive. The true senses awaken. For the first time, the Self can perceive the immense hidden beauty and love of Creation. The Self is now one with everything. The flowering of the Self begins. The Supreme Being begins expressing through the Self. Such a life is wonderful like a fairytale, having childlike freshness and joy, and no loneliness and boredom. The Self becomes free to soar high in the vast skies of Creation, and explore all hidden potential and beauty. This is the Shangri-La every Self seeks!!!

This book reveals the path of love and complete surrender. This path is a classical method. It was followed by many great Mystics of the past. They all entered into a loving relationship with the Supreme Being for experiencing oneness.

My Past Lives

HOW I BECAME A SEEKER:

I was a famous conqueror several hundred years ago. I was born into a royal family. I was personally tutored by a legendary teacher. I was blessed with a keen intelligence, great strategic competence, and enviable martial prowess. I always chose the mightiest challenges. I went from one conquest to another. I always won and never lost. Each win, against the most powerful of the day, grew my self-love and self-image further. I was so successful that I began seeing myself as the favored of the gods, and other people saw me that way as well. This brought my self-love and self-worship to its climax. I wanted more and more applause. My motivation was to be the greatest man who had ever lived. I had fine sensibilities. I performed many acts of benevolence and pioneered many social reforms and systems. I wanted only one thing more: immortalization of my Self. So conquering eternity became my last ambition. I thought I would find bliss and peace beyond that.

I went from one success to another at a very young age. Life kept on giving me all my wishes. I loved only one thing: myself. I thought I could conquer even eternity. Then the encounter with The Truth came. And I was humbled by the might of death. In those final moments my eyes opened. I realized there is a Supreme Reality beyond everything that no one can conquer. I surrendered. I fell in love with the Supreme Being. A metamorphic transformation happened. I became a Mystic. My last thoughts were that if I ever lived again, I would seek only the Supreme Truth.

I had many lives after that. I sought endlessly. I lived with many Great Masters. I received guidance from them. I renounced everything. There were lives during which I meditated from beginning to end. I meditated from deep love and complete devotion and had no attachment to anything else. Finally the Supreme Being revealed itself. My journey ended. I experienced reunion with the Supreme Reality. I refound bliss. I refound my peace. I refound ultimate freedom. I found true empowerment. I found the true meaning of life. I found real joy of living. I conquered my mind.

MORE ABOUT TRAVEL BEYOND MY TURNING POINT:

My urge was to find true happiness and self-freedom. My urge was to find my true Self. My urge was to know about the Supreme Power behind life. I had come to know that until I find them, I would not find peace. I had also come to know that they did not exist on the path I had followed. I had loved my self-image and its reflections up to the ultimate possible point, and not found what I sought. So from that turning point, 2300 years ago, I changed course toward The Supreme Truth. A new journey began.

Since I was a lover at heart, and I had found someone more lovable than my self-image -- I fell in love. A new love affair began: a love affair with the Supreme Being. Since my new love was with The Unknown, I wished to know more about it. This became my constant passion and gave me intense joy. I read everything I could about my love. I travelled everywhere, looking for someone who could tell me about my beloved. I sought nearness to everyone who described the beauties of my beloved. This de-anchored the immense and intense energy that I had generated and attached to my self-image. Now the whole of that energy flowed toward my new love: the Supreme Being. Never before had I felt such joy. I kept sinking deeper and deeper into it.

I would read endlessly about my beloved. I would sit near Masters for days, to hear just one word about my beloved. I would serve them from my heart, out of deep gratitude, yearning for an occasional glimpse of my love through them. The more love and surrender I transferred from the side of my self-image to love for the Supreme Being, the more joy I felt. The process continued for many lives. It was extreme joy. I never wanted it to end. I kept becoming inebriated with my new love. I would work with reason upon my mind to purify it, and prepare it like a vessel, to beg for more love from my Supreme Beloved. I was never satisfied. Gradually I carved an immense Begging Bowl out of it. For days on end I would beg for just a glimpse of my beloved. When it would be granted, I would beg for another glimpse. I had become a Mystic. This is what a Mystic is.

Many full lifetimes I sat in meditation and deep immersion into my beloved. The pain of icy cold conditions in high mountains, with hardly any clothing, and with no food for years, or with deathlike aloneness -- this pain did not matter at all, as it was for reunion with my beloved.

This is a classical path which was followed by seekers of the past. I have deeply experienced it. I have experienced the surrender of ultimate devotion through these practices. I have experienced the ultimate joy of this path.

I had had countless meetings with my beloved, the Supreme Being, before this life. Only one wish remained before Ultimate Dissolution into merging. For that, I wanted to live once more. Most lives when I was seeking, I was alone, away from the world with no family or society, just surviving on my love for the Supreme Being. I had become free from loneliness, sublimated my love, and found total faith in my love. The experience that remained was experiencing the beauty and potential of life beyond experiencing the Supreme Truth, and testing my love and faith for purity on the touchstone of life. I wished for it. I wanted to take it while living in a family amidst society. It is the most difficult test. This experience is the purpose of my present life.

So my travel toward Supreme Reality was from self-love and self-worship to complete surrender and selflessness in love with the Supreme Being. I wish to share here the essence of what I have experienced.

The happiness of love for the "I" is very small compared to the limitless bliss of love for the Supreme Being. The Supreme Reality is our true destination. We are in Creation to seek it.

My Present Life

MY RELATIONSHIP WITH THE SUPREME BEING:

I am in love with the Supreme Being. It is endless. I am in Creation for experiencing this love. I am on earth to experience this love. This relationship is the meaning of my life. Life after life I have lived for it. I have completely surrendered to it. My mind is now an empty vessel to receive what The Infinite wishes to pour in it every moment. I live my day to day life in this love and faith.

After countless lives in this love I have been pulled into oneness by The Infinite Unknowable. My relationship has flowered. Now there is no secret between us. In this state of pure consciousness, revealing experiences flow through my open mind. Knowing is now effortless and spontaneous. My understanding about life and things in this world has become very deep and clear, in this love.

MORE ABOUT MY EXPERIENCES:

I have deeply loved The Infinite for many lives -- up to total self-forgetfulness. I have deeply explored The Infinite for many lives, reasoning into endless mysteries, up to ultimate horizons. When I loved, I was loved back many times more. When I explored, I was revealed truths far beyond my questions. In my relationship, I have enjoyed experiencing the Supreme Being in every way, seeking constantly by devotion, prayer, meditation, exploration, and reasoning limitlessly. Gradually the illusion of separation created by my mind, within which I lived for eons, was dissolved.

ABOUT THIS LIFE:

My family and I lived in a small town at the foothills of the Himalayas. It was surrounded by forests and countryside. Such closeness to nature gave me a very enriching childhood. We would pick berries and flowers, watch and listen to wild birds, gather colorful feathers, catch butterflies, chase wild birds and animals, climb trees, search bushes, and collect rare looking stones.

I loved reading fables and fairytales. To me they felt real. Bedtime was special for me and my sister. We would look forward to it. Our maternal grandmother had an immense resource of stories. She never went to school, but her wisdom had no parallel. Her stories could fill up several books. I have not read as many even in "The Arabian Nights" or "Aesop's Fables." Her subjects always were Saints, Mystics, and legendary beings. All her stories were deeply inspiring, with a moral. We would go to sleep wondering and wishing. My faith was that I would meet these great beings in real life someday. I vividly remember how I once searched in the nearby forest, gathering hundreds of feathers, till I had a bagful. I wanted to build two large wings. I had read about the mythical Greek youth Icarus, and I wished to fly like him.

This kind of childhood gave me a strong foundation for the search of true reality. It was immensely complete and deeply satisfying.

Around the time I was six, the Supreme Being began revealing to me. The love-affair again began in this life. I did not know then that it was a relationship continuing from my past lives. This love again became my be-all and end-all after that. It has been like that ever since. Even as a child, nothing gave me more joy than being with the Supreme Being. While playing hide-and-seek, I would find a place where I could not be found for a long time. I could see and talk with the Supreme Being. I never felt alone. The Great Creator behind all the wonders I explored had become real for me. I felt immense love. I could communicate very freely. I would ask for my wishes. They would come true. I began inspiring other children to love God and experience miracles and joy.

My childhood beliefs and experiences had no connection with any religion. My family followed no religion. We went to a place of worship only infrequently. No one amongst us was prepared to accept things from outside our heart. We wanted our own experience of what we believed in. Our morality came from our own heart and its love. We accepted that all Prophets, Saints, and Mystics were Great Beings who had known the Supreme Reality and lived exalted lives. We respected all of them and read about their lives and paths.

My father had a postgraduate degree in Economics and was a senior government officer. He was a man of very few needs and simple habits. He was honest to the core, very principled, and willing to help everyone. He refused to believe what could not be experienced. This gave me very true basics in life. The greatest advice I got from him was: "Experience your own Truth." I can recall him reading lot of books on Spirituality, and on communication with higher spirits, when I was a child. But he kept them away from me and my younger sister. He never spoke about these books to us. He felt we would find our own truth when our time came.

My mother was completely devoted to looking after us. She constantly and openly declared that her one purpose in this life was to give birth to me. Much later, it was revealed to me that she had been my mother in many previous lives and belonged to a very high spiritual realm of souls. She was a being in whom mothering had evolved up to ultimate selflessness. This extended to anyone she met. From past lives with me, she was aware of my love for the Supreme Being and my endless seeking. She disclosed to me that I had gone further than any being had in this relationship with the Divine. She wanted me to share the joy I had found with the world. She had unquestioning faith in the Supreme Being. She also followed no religion. This upbringing gave me a totally free mind. I was left alone to seek and experience the truth of my reality and myself.

My father passed away in August 2004, in India. I was

near him. My mother passed away in December 2005 during a visit to the United States of America. While dying also they showed a peace and fearlessness that only knowing The Supreme Truth can give.

I was a good student. Learning was my passion. I had deep interest in relating Science to the Unknown. I would always search for the origin of things. An explorer, a maverick at heart, I always did things my own way. The beaten path never attracted me, nor did small challenges. I would score the highest on out of course exams. I could never be attentive in a class. I would be somewhere else -- deeply immersed in my own feelings and thoughts. I would later read the books on my own, and understand the subject to write my exams. Intuition guided me. I got good grades.

I graduated with a degree in Mechanical Engineering. I opted for jobs in Research and Development. I liked innovating. I used to custom design robots and machines to automate processes. My first job was with a British multinational corporation, where I worked for five years. Then I founded my own company. I continued with this work for about twelve years.

I married in the year 1979. My wife and I had lived together in many previous lives. I could not have been comfortable in such closeness with any other soul. She embodies selfless love, innocence, and directness. She gave me the stability and earthiness that I needed to live. Our greatest bond is that we are on the same path. We have co-evolved.

I have three children. The eldest is a son, and then two daughters. All of us have lived together many times in past lives and have come together again. All are evolved souls on the last lap of their journey of life.

My sister married in 1980. She has a son and a daughter. All three of them are also seekers of Reality, and co-traveling with me toward it. The caravan heading toward the Ultimate Destination is becoming larger every day. The Supreme Being has provided us with a very conducive environment for spiritual growth. So many souls familiar with each other from past lives, seeking and experiencing The Truth together ... this is heaven. The other common thing in us is that we all are aware we have a role to play as actors in the cosmic drama that we have chosen for our final performance on earth.

In 1990, when I was 34 years old, my relationship with the Supreme Being became fully active and very intense again. I knew my call had come. I felt the irresistible pull. I wanted to leave everything else. New transformations had begun. I was finding it difficult to continue with my profession. I now wanted only one thing: complete dissolution of all separation from The Infinite.

So we built a house in the Himalayas, in order to be alone. We moved there. I have been very fortunate that my family members have had the same seeking as mine. The place was spiritually very conducive. Our seeking became very intense. I would remain in communion with The Infinite most of the time. Then I would share the experiences with my family and answer their questions. The experiences with the Supreme Being extended to a pure relationship with Nature around me. I began experiencing the Supreme Being hidden in trees, wind, clouds, raindrops, mountains, stones, birds, streams, and butterflies -- it was like I was living the hide-and-seek of my childhood days all over again.

Several past lives were revealed to us during this period. My wife, son, daughters, sister, nephew, niece, and mother all were having similar experiences. We had been together in many previous lives. This helped us to understand and integrate many past qualities into ourselves. My father used to be along, but preferred to be alone. We knew he was evolving his relationship with the Supreme Being in his own way.

Around this time, I met a spiritually highly evolved being. Our meeting was another proof that Creation is not random, and it has a Supreme Intelligence directing it. His experiences with the Supreme Reality were unique. He shared them with me. No higher, point-blank demonstration, of Actualized Truth can be witnessed than the way he lived. Not a single thought or act of this great being ever deviated from true expression of the Supreme Truth. This ultimate teacher of Creation identified me, to help me crystallize my role here, and gave me the supreme management processes required to answer it. Interactions with him for fifteen years prepared me for the final act.

The phase of our lives in the Himalayas continued for almost seven years. It was now 1997. Gradually I returned to worldly activity. I now wanted to share with everyone about the Supreme Reality. I wanted everyone to experience loving the Supreme Being. I wanted everyone to know about their true relationship with The Infinite. I wanted them to find The Truth -- I wanted everyone to find their purpose and joy in life. Off and on I did a technical consultancy project for my livelihood.

During the next seven years, I loved the Supreme Being still deeper, and worked upon my mind deeply and endlessly. My freedom to love and trust further deepened. Life occasionally and appropriately tested the surrender of my mind in the material world. This was my touchstone to know how pure my awareness had become. I continued to share everything with my family and several others. I traveled a lot worldwide. I closely studied human nature, motivation, and behavior, wherever I went. I interacted with many. I wanted to know how people could be freed from ignorance regarding The Truth, and how they could be freed from the misery they were themselves causing in their lives. I wanted to share about the real joy of life.

Healing is another faculty the Supreme Being revealed to me. I have been learning it for almost twenty years now. I have acquired a deep clarity about the mind and the body. I have been able to heal many disorders, dysfunctions, and discomforts in myself and others. I take special care of these instruments of living -- they are the roots into life.

I have received so much love and so many resources from the Supreme Being that I have become a Love-bearer and a Truth-bearer. I am carrying this love and truth around to share it. I am carrying this message around to share it.

I wish to share everyone's true relationship with the Supreme Being. And why suffer in loneliness, pain, and misery? Peace is awaiting each one of us. Bliss is awaiting each one of us.

I began compiling this book from my experiences of several lives, fifteen years ago. Writing about such experiences in simple day to day language was not easy. Many times it looked complete but again it required more simplification. I have revised it countless times, many times with the help of the Supreme Being. I have here shared what have I received and understood about our true relationship with the Supreme Being, the purpose of life, and the way to live. This is my happiness. I have faith that I will be able to share this Reality with all during the coming time -- from the first being to the last being on earth!!!

P.S

I brought the manuscript of my book along when I immigrated to the USA in August 2009. I completed the finishing touches here. My coming to the USA had been revealed to me several times, ever since my childhood.

Many beings, including my mother, had visions about it. The Supreme Being kept bringing me here occasionally for almost 20 years, since my first visit in 1989. I have been guided to share the message of Truth from here, at a time when the world most needs it.

So I sold my home, gave away my belongings, and moved into this new world. Many have asked me why my message should be shared from the USA, I will answer this question further here.

It is the right place to answer my mission in life. I have spiritually grown up in the mysticism of the East, where I found my roots into the Infinite Source. To truly benefit mankind, the Inner Reality has to be reconciled with science to end the conflict. There is no country where the mind is as open to look into the new. The eagle in Creation symbolizes the highest flier into rarest realms, with the broadest vision, swiftness of movement, precision of action, and individuality; the USA has the spirit of this bird. For sharing about the new and unknown dimensions of life, the right platform is available here. My teacher told me that to open even the minds of the best inventors and explorers to The Ultimate Truth has remained the greatest of challenges in this world. But I am here, and I have begun my work as an unknown person with a small team: my wife, and my older daughter, whose call in life is the same. I know this team will grow in the future. There are many evolved souls here with whom I have lived in my past lives. This book will find them.

Our mission in life is to reveal The Supreme Truth so that the Self awakens to its true reality. There is no other way to solve the problems the world faces today. There is no other way the Self, Society, and the World will find true freedom and happiness. We wish to lay a strong foundation toward it during our life, from where it will continue to evolve.

About the Book

This book has the essence of my experiences with the Supreme Being. My seeking process extended over 2300 years. It has taken me fifteen years to compile it.

I have received so much love and truth during these experiences that I have become a Love-Bearer, a Truth-Bearer. To share my message, I felt a book would be the best medium.

I have here shared about the Supreme Being, the true relationship of the Self with the Supreme Being, the purpose of life, the bondage of the mind, the path to experience the Supreme Being, and true living.

The book will be relevant to all: seekers, non-seekers, even nonbelievers. For seekers it will clarify the path. For non-seekers, it will awaken a desire for the true quest. For nonbelievers, it will end conflict.

The theme of the book is love. It is in the language of the heart. The core emphasis is on love -- it being the key element in every seeking and on every path.

I have written this book in the same state of love, surrender, abandon, fascination, and naturalness, as I was immersed in during my experiences. While expressing about the Supreme Reality, randomness and repetition were unavoidable; this being a domain of the heart, language felt very limited. I have tried to convey the truest possible feeling and understanding from these experiences.

The purpose of the book is to reveal about the Supreme Being and the Supreme Reality. It will remind the Self about its original quest. After reading it, no Self can be the same again -- no Self can avoid falling in love with the True Reality. It will also help me to search for those souls I have a special bond with, from my past lives.

Have You Ever Thought?

Have you ever thought?
That Creation must have some purpose.
That everything in it would not be expressing so
much beauty without a very deep meaning.
That you also must have come here for a purpose.
What is it? What desire is hidden deep within
your heart that you do not know about? What is
keeping you out of real joy of living? Why peace is
still elusive?

Without knowing about your purpose for being here, you cannot give true meaning to your life. The constant turmoil of your Self is due to not knowing who you are, and why you are here.

It has been an eternity since you entered the journey through Creation. Deep within you are weary and want to arrive at the Ultimate Reality, to come to rest.

You want peace. You want happiness. You want complete

freedom of the Self. You want to be completely secure. You want complete clarity about life. You want a lasting meaning to live. You are struggling to find them. They do not exist outside the realm of True Reality.

You are living in fear and doubt. You are tense. You are in conflict with your source and life. You are suffering. You want some miracle to happen in your life.

You constantly attempt to hide and forget your endless turmoil. You create illusions of happiness and security by fooling your mind and senses. You clutch at beliefs that have no roots in the Ultimate Truth. You live in constant doubt but are not prepared to accept the difficult questions:

To whom are you lying?

Whose life are you continuously disordering?

When you are cheating your own Self, whom would you spare?

Peace and happiness are a quality of oneness with the Ultimate Truth. They are the most difficult to fake. Those who do not have them are selling them in the marketplace today. Nothing more remains to be plundered for money. But you are not aware that by fabricating false versions of peace and happiness, you have cut your last root into True Reality. Peace and happiness were the touchstone to test the real. Now how would you know the false from the real? Beyond such a critical point, only Nemesis can help to open human eyes.

Going against your purpose in Creation has caught up with you. Your Self is now expressing its deep unhappiness. Your false ways have overstressed you. The strain is showing as irrational fears, constant anxiety, purposelessness, dried up love, lack of trust, dysfunction, disorder, and disease. You think you are becoming more powerful and wise, but you are losing control over things in your reality. Disorder and disease are defying your knowledge and remedies. But you are still persisting with your ways and seeking relief in thoughts and acts having no roots in True Reality.

Life on earth is a very rare opportunity. It is a great chance to find your Self Truth and live it. No one can live here forever. You have to awaken to your true purpose for being here before your time ends. Where have the great mystics, philosophers, emperors, kings, warriors, conquerors, tyrants, scientists, poets, artists, and musicians gone once their time was over? Their wisdom, power, and wealth could not buy them one more moment when the end came. Only the ones who had found their True Reality were fulfilled, fearless, and blissful in the end.

Do not be fooled by any kind of power and wealth. What wisdom do lives of beings like even Alexander the Great reveal? He was respected as a living god, was the pupil of Aristotle, cut the Gordian knot, won Persia (the mightiest empire of the time), conquered and ruled most of the civilized world of his time, built the city of Alexandria, had immense wealth and treasure, and used to drink from a cup cut out of a priceless diamond. Do you know what his last feelings were?

"All is vanity."
Why?

He felt powerless when all his achievements and possessions could not help him to conquer death. He realized he had not arrived at the only eternal and powerful thing in Creation -- The Ultimate Truth.

Nothing else mattered to him, in the end. And to death he succumbed, as the most ordinary being.

In this world you also might be powerful, dictating the destinies of many, yet feeling the most insecure person yourself. You might be rich and famous and yet feeling incomplete. You might be very knowledgeable, but have never felt a moment of clarity and certainty. You might be very religious, and yet faith is elusive. You might be a guide to others, but do not know where to take your own life. You might have read lot of books on Self-Help and Self-Actualization but do not know your own Self. You might be showing paths to God, and God still is a mystery to you. In all these cases, you do not know The Truth yet.

You love your Self. You love life. You never want it to end. Be honest with yourself. Stop wasting your life. Seek to experience the Supreme Being. Know your Source. Know your Self-Truth. Experience it in yourself. It is your only source of real joy. It is the only realm where you can find your true happiness and peace. This life is the chance, and if you do not enter heaven while living here, you will not find it anywhere later when this life ends!!!

1

Supreme Being

Only the Supreme Being is.

Who is behind this vast Universe? Who created everything in it, and controls such an immense show? Who controls such an open-ended process? Who is behind the infinite forms and processes in it? Who can create and control from a grain of sand to the largest star? Who knows the entire past, present, and future in every moment? Who makes the sun rise and set and seasons change in perfect timing? Look at the countless stars in the night sky. Look at mountains, rivers, trees, plants, flowers, animals, birds, human beings. Everything is a Universe within a Universe. Everything is unique and beyond understanding. And yet, everything is related to one another and responding to one call. Everything is in harmony and living one order. Who is giving this call? Who loves everyone? Who guides everyone? Who controls everyone? Who evolves everyone? Who protects everyone? Who secures everyone? Who provides for everyone? Who ends everyone? Who scripted the endless story of life? Who reveals about it? Who directs all action? Who acts upon the script? Who wishes to know? Who feels? Who thinks? Who is the lover? Who is the loved? Who becomes happy? Who becomes sad? Who is the Self?

It is the Supreme Being -- the doer of everything!!!

We are conscious beings. We have a mind. We have superior powers. Rather than use them to seek the Supreme Reality, we have fallen into the folly of thinking we can completely control our lives and processes of nature. The infinitesimally small knowing we have acquired through religion and science has given us so much pride that we now think we will be able to control the Supreme Reality. What about our heartbeat, every breath, countless regulated processes within us and in the Universe, about which we may never know, and which keep us living? Without these unknown processes and order, the next moment would not come. Who decides when we have to be born and when we have to die? Who decides in every moment what is right for us and what is wrong? Who is taking us somewhere we do not even know about yet? Who either supports or opposes our intentions?

How much of the Supreme Being can we know and control? Can we ever become so wise and powerful as to completely run our lives in this Universe? Never ever will we be able to do it. The Supreme Being is infinite, open-ended, and indefinable. We are merely experiencing the wonders of what the Infinite Intelligence created and will continue to create as long as Creation lasts. Religion and science have only known what the Supreme Being chose to reveal from time to time. We just participate in this vast drama of life like a drop participates in a wave in the vast oceans. But this participation also is an expression of the Supreme Being.

After so many blessings, so much love and benevolence -- what a supreme proof of the immense and unconditional love of the Supreme Being: that we are allowed the freedom to disbelieve or ignore, even to disrespect the Supreme Power, as well as take pride in claiming credit for things we have not done.

Even after so much evidence, we are so unwise; we continue to ask for proof that The Supreme Being is. So many times, we have seen Divine might crumble our mightiest shelters. We have seen all our wisdom fail and prayer succeed, in life and death situations. And we have also seen help come out of nowhere to protect us, when we were all alone with no way out.

The Supreme Being is the Supreme Source: an unimaginable vast ocean of pure love, feeling, bliss, awareness, intelligence, power, potential, compassion, and countless unknown and unknowable qualities. No mind can ever become vast enough to contain it. It is all we know; all we will ever know; and all we will never know. Prophets, Saints, and Mystics from experiences during oneness with the Supreme Being have tried to reveal as much as a true mind can. But even this is infinitely little. In a state of deep awe and devotion, they wished to express something. But soon they felt how impossible it is. All of them indicated one thing: even if we continue describing Divine qualities for millions of ages, the unsaid and the unsayable will remain.

However, their experiences with The Infinite and revelations are very potent, to inspire other selves to seek The Indescribable Reality.

We may give the Supreme Being any name: God, Infinite, Creator, or something else. It does not matter. No experience or word can define the Supreme Being completely. We can express only a little about the Supreme Being from our experiences. The mind and the language limit us. But even that is enough to serve the purpose of awakening other selves to enter the true quest in life. Something has to be said to show the way toward the unknowable destination. Do not let words trap you in thoughts and ideas. Do not attempt to understand everything. Do not try to reason out everything. Feel with the heart. Have faith. If you can feel spontaneous awe, love, and urge to surrender arising within you when The Truth is revealed, the door to Supreme Reality has opened. If you allow this feeling to build up, it can become so powerful it will pull the Self into oneness with it.

The Supreme Being I have experienced is a lover, is beautiful, is a friend, is joyful, is playful like a child, loves living, is caring, is benevolent, reveals, guides, and creates the best conditions for seeking the Supreme Reality. It even gives misery, pain, disease, and death out of deep compassion and a purpose.

Creation displays the nature of the Supreme Being in the entire Universe. It displays its most exalted qualities within Prophets, Saints, Mystics, and Seekers.

No one can understand the Supreme Being. No one can define the Supreme Being. No one can possess the Supreme Being. We can love the Supreme Being. We can feel the Supreme Being. We can experience the Supreme Being. We can communicate with the Supreme Being. If it were not so, who responds when we pray? And who answers our questions when we have no clue and ask? So the Self can relate with the Supreme Being as it can with any other thing. And this relationship is real.

So, love the Supreme Being to become one. Love the Supreme Being above everything else. When a human heart loves, it begins going into deep oneness with what it loves. Love everything, because everything is the Supreme Being.

Do not hesitate. Do not feel embarrassed. Nothing about the Supreme Being is irrational. If there is anything irrational in this world, it is the limited basis a human mind uses for belief or disbelief. Unfortunately, most knowing about the Supreme Being and Reality is just a product of thought and imagination, and is fragmentary. Know about the Supreme Being from a being who has experienced oneness, and you will know the difference.

Evidence of what powerful transformation happens within the Self after experiencing the Supreme Being can be seen by knowing about the lives of Saints, Prophets, and Mystics. They all lived from their relationship with the Supreme Being. Their lives are a true demonstration of the Self's true relationship with the Supreme Being.

The Supreme Being is the Original Reality and the true home of the Self. The Self came into Creation from oneness with it and will return to it one day. The world is a beautiful home for the Self, but temporary. This home can become blissful and comfortable only if its temporariness is realized. The Self may feel secure in this worldly home and its reality, but this security is also temporary and a belief. Life is meant to be a bridge -- a bridge the Self has to use to cross over into Supreme Reality: the Real Home.

The Supreme Being also has a heart and is the ultimate lover. Why else would it respond to the love of a seeker? I have been in a love affair with the Supreme Being and have personally experienced it. No climax of life is greater than being accepted by the Supreme Being. No price is too high for a reunion. The ecstasy of meeting is beyond description.

I surrendered everything I had in this love, and have never regretted it. I could surrender it many times over for just one meeting.

The Supreme Being has to be experienced both within, and in real life -- otherwise any experience is incomplete. No Self can return home to Absolute Merging with the Supreme Being without that.

2

Supreme Truth

Without knowing about the Supreme Truth, the Self cannot seek to experience it.

How can you experience what you do not know about? You cannot. Know about the Supreme Being and the Supreme Reality in order to seek.

The Supreme Being is the only Reality. Everything in Creation is its expression. Creation arose out of love: the love of the Supreme Being for itself, the love for self-knowing and experiencing. From this desire began the grand drama of life. A duality arose in the Supreme Consciousness. Opposites were required for organizing life and experiencing it. The Supreme Being divided into the lover and the loved; the experiencer and the experienced; the seeker and the sought. Within the Infinite Nothingness a massive churning and energization began. Gradually the immense ocean of energy became cosmic plasma, in which basic elements began organizing. The Supreme Being's infinite qualities began separating. Over eons, conscious life forms appeared. After eons more, consciousness arrived at the stage of an individualized Self, which could feel and think. So the origin of Creation was in love, and its purpose is love. The true quest of the Self in Creation is to experience the Supreme Reality.

The Self is now a mind. It has forgotten its original reality. It is difficult for it to accept the Original Oneness. The Self now accepts only phenomenal reality as real. It can only understand things in a subject-object relationship. The Self thinks the Ultimate Reality is on a continuum with its present reality. It thinks it will someday arrive there by processes of its mind. Mind is an instrument that can understand only duality. It does not exist within oneness. The Supreme Truth transcends duality. The logical process of subdividing things and analysis, or synthesis from understood parts to understand The Whole, does not work in the realm of Supreme Truth. It has infinite dimensions. Individual dimensions can be explored and understood separately, but Supreme Reality cannot be projected or assembled from parts. Since the beginning of time, all beings that have ever arrived back at the Original Reality have transcended their minds.

Till the Self sees its present reality is not The Truth, it will not seek beyond. Pain and misery are essential to disillusion and detach the Self from present reality. Feelings of restlessness, insecurity, loneliness, meaninglessness, boredom; the urge for unlimited power and freedom; excessive self-love and pride; knowing a lot and yet being confused; having a Faith and yet being fearful; understanding the futility of superficial living and yet not ready to let go -- are all signs that show the Self is ripening, and the stage of a seeker is near. They show a stage is approaching where the Self will accept that it does not yet know The Truth; and that its present way of living is not going there. This is the stage where deeper questions about life will arise, and passion for the answers will take control of the mind. Then nothing else will matter but search for the Supreme Truth. But never forget -- only with love and faith can the Self enter the Supreme Realm.

Love brought the Self into Creation. Only love can take it home. If you have not experienced the Supreme Being yet, your love is still not total. This means you have not known about the Supreme Being enough to fall in love and surrender completely. Till the Self becomes one with the Supreme Being, it will not arrive there.

First know about the Supreme Being up to a point where the mind accepts.

Know about the Supreme Being from a being who has experienced it. Revelation is guidance from the Supreme Being. Without revelation, no one in the world can ever know and experience the Supreme Truth. The God that the Self has imagined with the mind, from past beliefs, cannot be found. Revelation is the Supreme Being's help to put the Self on the path toward reunion. Only the Supreme Being can show the way to itself. Prophets, Saints, and Mystics express from spontaneous Revelation they receive in a state of perpetual oneness with the Supreme Being.

The Supreme Being occasionally gives deeper revelations about Reality for evolving a higher awareness and actualization in the world. Through miracles, it induces a desire in the Self to seek the Supreme Reality.

The Self has loved so many things, but never felt pangs for the Supreme Being and Reality. Revelation awakens the desire to seek the Supreme Being.

The Self's core question is: WHO AM I?

Every Self is a unique quality of the Supreme Being that has separated when Creation began. We can know the answer to this question only when we become one with the Supreme Being.

Earth is a physical plane. Energy here is in a state of dense matter because of slower vibration rates. Even the mind and thought have a lower vibration rate than in higher spiritual realms. But life here is a rare opportunity to experience self-knowing and liberation. Living on a material plane gives a deeper experience than do purely thought and spiritual planes. Separation of the Self from its source is more pronounced here. Ignorance is deeper. Understanding about Reality is coarse. There is more doubt. The Self has to go through more pain and misery. The Self cannot dissolve doubt by thought alone here. To experience the Supreme Reality here requires deep love and faith, but once found, it liberates the Self completely.

Never seek to skip physical experience by escaping into thought planes or manipulating physical reality by laws of higher planes. Doing so will decrease the depth of experience and not liberate completely. This is why Great Spiritual Masters discourage causing miracles, and recommend living by rules of the physical while on earth. Using spiritual powers for relief is like playing hide-and-seek with x-ray vision. It would be cheating, and no fun at all. Spontaneous miracles happen around people on the path. They do not cause them. Masters occasionally cause miracles, but they do so with the sanction of the Supreme Being. Only they are aware when it is right.

What if you knew that human life did not happen to you by chance -- if you knew how much you wanted to be here? If you knew you were one of the countless souls urging to live; if you knew your original urge can most deeply be realized in this world only; if you knew that the bridge to eternal bliss is physical experience of the Supreme Being? You would hold this chance with both hands. From this very moment, you would put your entire soul into knowing who you are.

Life began as a process toward self-knowing. Become free of any guilt that you were expelled from any heaven. We can see physical proof of the desire to live everywhere around us. Look at any living thing in the world. What do we see? Self love. The urge to keep on living. The urge to thrive. The urge to excel. Pain and misery are part of the experience we are here for. Without them, the Self would never have become a seeker of True Reality. Knowing The Truth makes the Self accept the complete Reality.

The Self was not expelled from any heaven as a punishment. Life began from a spontaneous urge. What does so much beauty in nature indicate? What does so many flowers blooming indicate? What does so many birds singing indicate? What does human beings seeking to live forever indicate? If Creation was a prison, nature would not be celebrating. The bondage of the Self is ignorance of Supreme Reality, and not Reality of the world.

The Earth Plane is ripe for An Awakening to the next level of consciousness. The pangs for it are being felt by many human beings. Selves and processes are crying for a Metamorphosis to a new and higher Reality.

3

Great Beings

Prophets, Messiahs, and Saints were one with the Supreme Being. Knowing what they said about the Supreme Truth, and the way they lived when they were here, is very inspiring and liberating on the path. Knowing how deeply they loved the Supreme Being and how surrendered they were to the Supreme Being inspires the Self in seeking. You can catch the flame of true love from them, even if they are long gone from here. The power and presence of an awakened being is eternal. Besides, they respond if called to help, even now.

The Great Beings were expressing the Supreme Being from oneness with it. They saw the Supreme Being within everything in Creation, and loved it. So powerful were their demonstrations of the Supreme Truth that they caused a tremendous awakening in human consciousness.

There were a lot of qualities common in all the Great Beings. They all had become one with the Supreme Being. They all were expressing the nature of the Supreme Being. They all were unique. They all were selfless. They all had limitless love, faith, and courage. They all were detached from material things, but respected physical life. They all challenged living from the past. They all wished to free the human mind from ignorance of the Supreme Truth. They all revealed the Supreme Truth in a contemporary, more evolved, and simpler form. They all were accepted by very few people in their time. They all were violently opposed by existing religions of the time.

The Self is awed by greatness. It identifies with someone whose acts inspire it. It draws inspiration and guidance from greatness, to find its own reality. Heroes from the past, fictional super-beings, legendary lovers, philosophers, great emperors, explorers, scientists, athletes, and even actors have been idols in this world. The qualities that the Self loves in others, it wishes for. Those qualities already exist as a potential within the Self, otherwise it would not be attracted toward them. Knowing about the lives of Prophets, Messiahs, and Saints has the same kind of effect. This knowledge touches the core of the Self. It inspires the Self to seek the Supreme Being. It also helps a Self already on the path. Such a Self's love and faith increase further. The path becomes clearer.

Scriptures contain revelations about the Supreme Being from experiences of these Great Beings. But you cannot read and know the meanings of their content like ordinary books. There meanings have infinite dimensions, which evolve with time. Only enlightened Masters can see these dimensions and reflect their truth to you. Only they can convert it to right guidance for you. When unenlightened priests interpret Scriptures, they become religious dogma.

When scholars research scriptures, they disintegrate their wholeness and spirit. In both cases, The Truth becomes contaminated with the human mind, and inferior to it.

Another very significant point is that the same Truth has been revealed by Prophets, Saints, and Mystics of different times. I could see one consistent Truth revealed by all of them. I could see no conflict or contradiction between any of them. Apparent differences are there, because each of them was answering a different stage of evolution of the mind. Also, each of them had a unique individuality, meant to express The Truth in a way most relevant to that time.

Each one of us was born in a religion. That gave us our first knowing about the Supreme Being. Religion and holy books laid a foundation in us, for seeking the Supreme Being later. Every Self begins from reverence, out of fear of the Supreme Being. The core fear is of death, and what will happen to us after death. The Self prays to feel secure, and asks for favors that make it happy. At the next stage, the heart gets involved. The Self begins relating with the Supreme Being through devotion and worship. As the Self matures, it wants an actual experience of the Supreme Being. Now it seeks a deeper knowing and a path. At this stage, the Self needs to become free of all religious conditioning from the past to have its own experience. A seeker at this stage often appears as a rebel disrespecting religion. This is not true. It is a normal stage to experience in seeking. At this stage a Master is required. The Master can bring out the true meaning of past spiritual knowledge to the Self. Truth is hidden within it, like gold in sand. Understanding is required now, in addition to reverence. Beyond experiencing the Supreme Being, the Self comes to know the Supreme Truth is one and can never change, and that its expressions have to evolve with time like everything else.

To understand the true meaning of your scripture, relate with the Great Being of your religion. You will begin receiving intuitive guidance. Only this process can renew, reveal, and develop the true potential of the religion you are following.

I have loved all the Great Masters. I have loved them as great expressions of the Supreme Being. They have responded to me. I have received love, guidance, and blessings from them, through deep communion.

But for the help of the Great Beings I would never have found the Supreme Being.

4

True Destination

The Truth is that there is only one destination:
The Supreme Being. The Self is in Creation to
arrive there. Everything in Creation is seeking it.
It is the original Reality whence the Self began
its journey eons ago. It is the ultimate destination
where this journey will end -- and the Self will
awaken to the Supreme Reality.

Life cannot be lived without a destination. Desire, destination, and purpose sustain life. Without them there can be no beginning, no love, no will, no energy, no flow, no movement, no seeking, no experience, no knowing, no joy, no completion, and no end. Creation began from a desire toward an ultimate destination: the Original Desire. The destination to arrive at was the Supreme Reality. It is the true destination of the Self.

The Self has journeyed for many lives toward its true destination, without being aware. In this unaware phase of evolution, the Self is kept on the path by destiny -- the Self has no free will. The Self thinks it is making its choices, but that is not a reality. Creation knows what will tempt the Self and puts that very thing in front of it. The Self can choose nothing else. The choice is a compulsion of the Self. The mind will accept nothing else. From a limited consciousness and understanding the Self thinks it chose what it wanted from many things. This is why destiny of a Self in this stage can be predicted quite accurately. Astrology, Numerology, and Palmistry would not work without these constraints. That is why the destiny of an enlightened being cannot be predicted. Such Selves have real free will.

The first true choice the Self will ever make is leaving the illusions of the material world for seeking the Supreme Being. The first step toward this destination is from free will. For the first time, you will taste true freedom. Power is not required to protect this freedom. You will know when you experience it. Arguments and debates at this stage would be futile. If you disagree, maintain your present understanding and continue to live the way you are, till you feel the purposelessness of not having a true destination, and until you feel the bondage and burden of your mind.

One day the Self will come to know that, in reality, behind the pangs of its heart for everything it has ever loved was hidden just one love: love for oneness with the Supreme Being, and the urge to arrive at the Supreme Reality. That is why all its apparently self-chosen destinations gave it no happiness for long.

Actually the Self is gasping for the Supreme Reality like a fish gasps for water. The Self's present life and environment are not the water of life for it. The Self has to awaken to its true quest for the real destination: The Supreme Being. Only on the path toward it will the Self find joy, freedom, vitality, and real expression. The Self has to begin loving the Supreme Being. That is its True Home -- its eternal and real habitat.

You might have given a form to the Supreme Being in your mind from your beliefs, imagination, and reasoning. You fear the Supreme Being. You pray to the Supreme Being for help when nothing works. You might even be one who denies the Supreme Being. Whatever way you relate, it is the center of your existence. Experiencing the Supreme Reality will always remain your core urge, regardless how much material attachments in life pull you away from it. In fact it is to secure the self-attachments that the need to know the Supreme Being first arose. Whether it is religion or science, at the deepest level, the subject is eventually the Supreme Reality. It continues to be a mystery for both seekers and non-seekers. Till the ultimate is experienced, no mind can be certain and come to rest. The Supreme Being is your soul-urge. The Supreme Being is your True Destination.

The process toward the Supreme Destination requires ultimate devotion, hard work, and patience. All the love of your heart, and unwavering faith, are forerunners of such an experience. First, a life dedicated to cultivating these innermost Self-qualities is essential. No shortcuts will do. Partial commitment, or off and on practices, will lead nowhere. A complete price has to be paid. The surrender to the Supreme Being has to be total. The mind-body vessel needs a lot of preparation before it can actually experience the Divine. It has taken seekers lifetimes of total devotion, unquestioning faith, and hard work to arrive at states where true experiences began. The processes that the Mystics and saints from the past went through for a communion are proof of what it involves. It took me almost 1500 years of single-minded devotion in the aware stage before I had my first deep communion. Just imagine the additional social opposition seekers of the past struggled against. They had to withdraw from all else, surrender all attachment, and seek aloneness by going to mountains and forests. Their love for the Supreme Being was so pure and deep that they continued seeking even when threatened with death. Seekers still face opposition, but it is not as violent.

The length of the true seeking process should not discourage you. A Self drawn to seeking Reality is already quite ripe, and has developed faculties and the strength. It is aware of its feelings, thoughts, and choices, having lived a more conscious life. The inner call cannot be heard otherwise. Now the wish is for the last lap toward experiencing the Supreme Being. Even if spiritual experiences take time, the Self immediately becomes more aware, free, and happy.

The Self needs to become aware of a lot of things about this destination, before entering the path of serious seeking toward it. The Supreme Being is no ordinary destination. All seeking the Self has experienced so far has been from a known thing to known thing. This situation is different. Here, point A can be defined but point B is unknowable. Fears and doubts about this unknown Reality are much stronger. The Self will require unlimited love and faith for journeying in this domain.

Knowing about the destination is the first step as is the case in other areas of life -- because feeling love for the destination is the core of every seeking. Paths can be many. The Self has to choose one closest to its heart. Knowing about the destination is always the right beginning. If knowing about it gives happiness, the Self is ready. Knowing will also dissolve doubts and apprehensions arising from past beliefs about the new and unknown Reality.

In reality, between the Self and the Supreme Being there is no separation or distance. But the nature of the mind is such it thinks there is a distance to be traveled. So to dissolve this illusion, the Self will have to become a seeker, make the Supreme Being its destination, fall in love, and choose a path and journey. Someday, spontaneously, the oneness happens. Just knowing the Ultimate Truth is not the end. The Self has to live toward it and experience all the stages of it to make it a reality.

The first experience of Bliss is experienced when the Self comes to know about its real destination. When the Self steps on to the path toward it, the joyous feeling is ever-increasing. Then the Self can live for nothing else.

Know about the true destination; choose a path closest to your heart, and step onto the path.

5

Guru

A Guru is a being who is one with the Supreme Being. The Guru is expressing the Supreme Being. When a seeker's prayers are heard, the Supreme Being sends a Guru. As one lamp lights another, the seeker can pick up the spiritual flame from the Guru's Divine Flame.

A Guru is a being who exists at the interface of human and divine. A Guru is simultaneously of this world and not of this world. Only true seekers who have been on the path know how great a blessing it is when the Supreme Being blesses a Self with a Guru. A Guru appears when the prayers of a seeker are heard. It is the response of the Supreme Being to your love.

The Ultimate Guru is the Supreme Being. All Gurus bear the Supreme Being's love and message for delivery in Creation. Gurus are aware and have the deep humility that they do not possess what they are sharing. Gurus are true hollow reeds through which The Divine is expressing itself.

A Guru is everything the Supreme Being is, so much at one is the Guru with the Supreme Being. But the Guru has one thing that even the Supreme Being does not have: A HUMAN HEART. A Guru can feel your pain and wants to stake everything to free you from it forever. A Guru has no other motive. When you allow the Guru to help you, the Guru is deeply thankful to Creation.

In a Guru, the Divine Flame is burning bright. Without this illumination, no Self can find its way to the Supreme Realm of bliss, which is across endless, dark, deep, unknown realms of Creation. To arrive there, the seeker has to cross this fearful darkness. Only the Guru's lamp can show the way there; only the Guru's voice can guide where even light cannot go. No one else can go there with you. There are no footprints of earlier seekers there that you can follow. The Guru first shines the light of wisdom and reason into the dark recesses of the seeker's mind. This helps the seeker to see inside the mind, clear the filth of lifetimes, cleanse all impurities, and become free of illusions and fears. As the mind becomes empty and childlike, the Guru inspires it with the true desire for the Supreme Being.

Gurus are the deepest learners of the Supreme Reality. They never stop learning till the end. They remain students. They do not conclude. Their expression about The Truth remains fresh and ever-excelling. They are unique. Never compare one Guru to another.

Gurus live in the Bliss and contentment of oneness with the Supreme Being. They are living purely as their selves, and sharing spontaneously like the Sun, moon, stars, rivers, clouds, winds, trees, animals, and birds in harmony with nature.

You can never find a Guru. The mind has no faculty to identify a Guru. A Guru finds you. Only the Supreme Being knows your true Guru. When you become a seeker, just pray to the Supreme Being for guidance, and a Guru will appear. You will see how irresistible your Guru is to you. You will spontaneously fall in love. Barriers will melt.

Gurus know your Self more than you know it. They love you long before you love your Self. They have faith in you long before you have faith in your Self. That is why they are more concerned about you than you are about your Self. Being near them, the miracle begins to happen. You begin becoming your true Self. The Guru is adding nothing to you, but is just helping you to become free from what is not your Self. The Guru has no motives other than helping you to find the Supreme Reality.

Gurus are not randomly sent to a seeker. A Guru is a being with whom you have a bond from countless past lives. A Guru might have been a parent, sibling, friend, or teacher in a past life. The level of familiarity is very deep, and it is required to accept and receive Truth. A Guru has lot of inherent qualities in common with you. What attracts you to a Guru is that the Guru is expressing what you have as a potential to be developed. The same Truth is shared by all Gurus, but the Guru you will be attracted to will be saying it in the way that is closest to your heart.

There are two ultimate love affairs in Creation: one with the Guru, and the other with the Supreme Being. At a deeper level they are the same love affair. The life of a Guru is expressing Reality. It is demonstrating it. This expressed beauty becomes irresistible to the Self. As with every other love affair, everyone does not get attracted toward everyone else. You will fall in love with this being who, in addition to being exalted, is unique to you. This being will be the ultimate in beauty to you. The love of a Guru for you is no less. A Guru wishes to give you everything: all the love, all the spiritual wealth, all the wisdom, the entirety of Creation, and make sure you find the bliss of ultimate freedom, and do not suffer any more. You will also feel like loving the Guru more than anything, and will wish to give everything. It is wonderful and an ecstasy to experience a love-affair that is so exalted. A relationship with a Guru is the ultimate experience in love. It is an experience of purest love possible in life, completely selfless love, a love that is unconditional. You search for a soul mate, and the Guru is your ultimate soul mate. What an experience when two hearts wish to beat in one rhythm! What better company than being co-travelers toward the Supreme Reality? A human heart becomes inebriated with love in this relationship and wishes for nothing more. Union with the Supreme Being happens spontaneously in such exalted dynamics of love.

In all your worldly love affairs so far, lovers have tried to use you for their happiness and take something away from you. A love affair with the Guru will be the first where the lover wishes to give everything to you and exalt you to Supremeness.

Are Gurus required?

Most minds today reason they are not required. The easy availability of knowledge in Self-help and How-to books has caused a belief that the Ultimate Reality can be reduced to a workbook. In the initial stages, the Self can know a few secrets about life from here and there, but experiencing the Supreme Being is a different realm.

Why does the Self not learn without, teachers, instructors, and coaches in all areas of life, by the same reasoning? Why send kids to school for learning? Why not give Self-help books to them and leave them on their own to graduate? Why is a coach needed to teach a stroke of tennis or golf? Try learning it yourself, and you will know. I play tennis and I know. Try learning swimming, driving, flying, or anything by yourself, and you will have the answer. When, while acquiring simple skills, the Self feels the need for a guide, how can the Self make a path toward an Infinite Unknown it has no clue about? All clues from Self-help books are not even one piece in the Infinite Jigsaw Puzzle of the search for the Supreme Reality. Besides, most books about The Truth have been written by people who have not travelled the path all the way to the destination. It is very simple and direct to experience the Truth by being near a being who is one with it.

Very little can be said or written about, the Supreme Reality. Besides, it is happening, and is available only in the present moment always. The spiritual flame can only be caught in the present moment. Reading about religion can only prepare you for becoming a seeker. The Truth has to be felt and received in a living process. Only a flame can light another flame -- a picture or description of a flame will do nothing. What makes up a flame can be understood from chemistry, but an experience of its light and warmth is different. Light a candle, go to a dark room, and sit there just watching the flame. The effect is very different from reading about the constituents of a flame and about combustion in a book. Even experimenting with a flame does not reveal the complete reality. There is a lot beyond science and knowledge that is hidden in every phenomenon. In a true process, feeling precedes understanding.

Remember always, the scientific process toward knowledge through experiment, observation, and conclusion does not work in seeking the Supreme Being. In science you conclude at the end; in this search you have to begin from complete faith. Here feeling, love, and faith cause a state of total acceptance: then experience happens. In science you are searching for something you do not know exists. Here you accept the Supreme Reality and seek only an experience. This process is unknown to you. You know only about learning with the mind -- not without the mind. Without a Guru, you will get lost within your mind and never be able to transcend it.

Teachers give what they know from what they have been taught, and from what they have tried. Coaches give their practiced skills. Gurus live in oneness with the Supreme Being and share like a flame. A Guru loves you, and helps you to prepare to receive the Truth. The Supreme Reality gets expressed in their way of living and does something more powerful than the spoken word. This sharing is very subtle. Be near such a being for a few moments, and you will know.

Do not let your pride get in the way. You want to remain in control. In all other learning relationships you remain in control. With a Guru, learning begins with surrender of control. How else will you become free of the mind? Your mind does not accept it.

You are scared of a Guru because you do not wish to shed your false Self. You are attached to it. You have also hidden so much within your mind you do not wish to see, and which no one else knows. There are parts of your Self you dislike and have rejected. You do not want all this content to come into conscious reality. You know that in order to become free, these areas will have to be worked upon. The Guru can see through your mind. The Guru will reveal these things to you. This fear makes you reason that a Guru is not required. When things do not work after you try on your own, you accept that Gurus are required, but you still wish to avail yourself of guidance from a distance. Again, you want to be in control. It is only the passion of an advanced seeker that burns down this resistance. You cannot remain stuck at this point in time. Until you carve out a vessel to receive -- what will the Supreme Reality pour into? A Guru helps you with this process of preparation.

A Guru is your best friend. You can share anything with a Guru. You have lived so many intimate lives together before. Gurus remain connected with you regardless of distance and time -- so much so that the relationship continues on different planes of existence, even across the barriers of life and death. A lot of inner guidance you receive is from such beings, without your knowing.

Doubt does not end even after experiencing the Supreme Being many times. The mind continues to doubt -- was my experience real? Here again, only a Guru can help. From where else will you get the proof that silences the mind forever?

The point is not whether you need a Guru or not; it is when will your time come to enter the realm of bliss, and Creation bless you with one?

6

Love

Love is the Supreme Being. Love is the Supreme Reality. Love is the Self. Love is the path to the Supreme Being. Love is bliss on the path. Love is the bliss of ultimate merging. Love is everything in Creation.
If there were no love there would be no Self, no Creation, and no life.
Love begins everything and love ends everything. Love is the Supreme Power.

Love is the substance everything is made of. Love is the core quality of everything. It is the ultimate beauty. It is the core feeling. It is the ultimate power. It is the urge for experience. It is the urge for expression. It is the urge for oneness. It is the urge for merging. It is the urge for dissolution. Nothing is possible without love. Creation arose out of love. Creation survives on love. Love is evolving and excelling everything in Creation toward the Supreme Reality.

The Supreme Being cannot be experienced without love. Only love has the magnetism by which the Self can pull even the Supreme Being. Paths and methods mean nothing till love is felt. It is only in love that you are prepared even to die for an experience. This intensity of feeling is essential on the path toward the Supreme Being. Without love, the Self cannot find the feeling and the courage required on the path: to accept the Supreme Being, seek the Supreme Being, surrender to the Supreme Being, and dissolve into the Supreme Being. To express love for the Supreme Being in this world requires a lot of courage. To experience the Supreme Being requires ultimate courage. Love makes the Self transcend all fears and find this courage. Fears do not exist where love exists. Love transforms fear into faith. Only with courage of love can you go near what you fear, experience its reality, and become free.

Without love, faith cannot survive. Love gives faith the stability to be unwavering. Love gives faith the strength of ultimate reason. Love causes fearlessness, and faith becomes ultimate. Faith is the ultimate quality of love. Love asks for no whys. It requires no reason. Its reason is feeling. Its reason is of the heart. Its reason is innocent. Its reason is childlike. Its reason is self-evident. Its reason is that Ultimate. Creation and life stand on such a reason. The faith of love asks no questions, sets no conditions. You may approach faith from love or approach love from faith. After a stage, both merge into absolute love. Both become complete together.

No mind can contain love. Love is too vast. So the mind begins dissolving in love. It becomes silent and opens up when love arises. Never try to understand love -- feel it, instead. If you cannot feel love, catch it like a flame from someone who truly loves. It is love that awakens supreme wisdom and understanding. Finding love is essential before starting on the path toward the Supreme Being.

To experience the Supreme Being, the Self will have to find the feeling of love. The heart is its source. A relationship of love with the Supreme Being is essential for experiencing oneness with it. The Supreme Being will immediately begin reaching out. The Supreme Being is the greatest lover. The Supreme Being is expressing its love in Creation also. The whole Creation begins relating to, guiding, and supporting a Self in a love-affair with the Supreme Being. Limitless joy arises, life begins flowering, bliss is felt, peace is felt. Only love can cause the metamorphosis required in the Self to experience the Supreme Reality. Only by love the Self can become what it truly is.

Experiencing the Supreme Being requires complete surrender of the "I," and freedom from the illusions of the mind. Only in love does the Self wish to surrender its "I." Only in love does the Self wish to surrender its dearest thing: pride. Only in love does the Self wish to pay any price. This power of love brings humility and freedom to the Self. The Self becomes free of fear, doubt, and conflicts, which are the things that keep the Self separated from the Supreme Being and ecstasy of reunion.

Love is the principal vibrational frequency. It is the highest vibrational frequency in Creation. It is the frequency of the Divine heart. So love the Supreme Being, love Creation, love Life, love the Family, love Society, love the Self -- and you will begin vibrating at the same frequency. An experience of the Supreme Being will spontaneously happen. Nothing else is when love is. And when there is nothing else, only the Supreme Being is.

Your fear is that love is irrational. In an unaware Self, it is. Love is no longer irrational once the Self awakens to Reality. It is supra-rational. The love of an awakened Self includes its reason. It includes its balance and control. Love is double-edged in an unaware Self. It is fire. It is too mighty to be handled. It is emotional energy difficult to tame. It can create as well as destroy. It can free as well as bind. It can melt illusion and also cause illusion. It depends upon whether love is selfless or self-centered. Detached love is supreme. Attached love causes bondage. Reason can only separate one from the other. Do not make the mistake of seeing emotional love as Love. Emotional love is a temporary, transient expression of love, and is conditional. In it the Self seeks only gratification of a need. Emotional love has its role in life, but eventually love has to become free of emotions in order to become Supreme.

The Self is wounded and worn out from emotional shocks in so many lives; it needs deep healing. Only love will heal the Self. It is the ultimate healer. All wounds and pains melt away in it. The heart revives. Innocence is re-found. Childlike interest in life revives. Conflict, disorder, and disease spontaneously resolve in love. The mind and the body both regain health. Love sees only beauty. It sees no ugliness. It shares, to free the Self from what is not the Self' to liberate this beauty, and make the Self whole and happy.

Love awakens true compassion. It exalts compassion from being just an emotion out of moral beliefs and guilt to pure empathy. The selflessness and oneness with everything that love brings exalts compassion to its ultimate expression. Prophets, Messiahs, and Saints displayed it.

The purpose of love is the original purpose of Creation. It wishes to exalt the Self to its supreme quality. Love is so powerful and magical -- the same mind that initially defends against everything, and resists opening up and letting go, now feels happiest while surrendering everything it gathered and protected for moving ahead. The process of love is very beautiful. Test it anywhere in life; it will work. If something is not working in life, then love is the missing ingredient. Add it and see.

To catch the flame of love, observe the Supreme Being's expressions in Creation. The Supreme Being is the greatest lover. Know about the lives of Prophets, Messiahs, Saints, and Mystics. Know about legendary lovers. Know about true love from their expressions of love.

7

Heart

Till the Self finds its heart, it will not be able to experience the Supreme Being.

Heart is the center of the being. It is the innermost part of the Self that feels. It gives the call of the true Self. It is the unique Self-nature. It is the Self's natural and spontaneous response in the moment. The Self lives from the heart only -- both when it is a child, and after it becomes enlightened.

Nature lives from its heart. Observe it and you will know what living from the heart means. Nature lives from feeling. Nature is instinctive. Nature has pure responses. Nature is total when it responds. At other times it is in pure silence. The response of anything in nature is the response of Creation as a whole. A bird wants to sing, or fly from one branch to another; it expresses that feeling with its total Self. If it is hungry and an insect flies, it instinctively goes for it. There is complete attention and expression of the instinct. But when satisfied, it sits in contentment and harmony. This peaceful resting phase is full of contentment after the total expression. Birds and animals give mating calls at a certain time of the year. The courtship and the sex act is a total and pure expression of the heart. They do not have sex constantly on their minds for pleasure and diversion. When faced with real danger they instinctively respond. They do not live in fear day and night about what will happen. Nothing in nature doubts its ability. Everything in nature is always attentive and participating in living. Mountains, glaciers, forests, rivers, trees, animals, birds, insects, plants, and flowers are all expressing their naturalness, responding to change, evolving, and excelling. There is no residual tension or vengeance in nature after an expression. Even when an expression is blocked, the buildup of energy and release is toward restoration of harmony.

In Creation a tiger behaves like a tiger, an eagle like an eagle, a flower like a flower, a plant like a plant, a tree like a tree, a river like a river, the sun like the sun, a cloud like a cloud, the earth like the earth, the ocean like an ocean. Their behavior expresses their true Self. The only exception is the human Self. It behaves like someone else for approval of others and reflected happiness. It does not live from its heart at all. Human motives are complex. They arise not from the heart and pure desire, but from emotional attachments and mind states. Memories of pleasure and pain from the past constantly define human happiness. The un-awakened Self is an image constructed from past memories in which the Self takes pride. Its happiness depends upon the conditioning of its mind. Its relationship with God and holy practices are also motivated by mind states of: fear of death, insecurity, pain and misery, greed, spiritual pride. The genuine urges of the heart are missing in most human expression.

As a child, the Self lived from its heart. It could imagine and have faith in anything. Every fairytale it read was enjoyable and felt real. It would imagine the story coming true in life. In the imagination were fairies and angels. The Self wished to fly like the birds and swim like the fish and imagined doing these things. That is why life was so joyful. As it grew up and became worldly-wise, it began losing faith in its own heart, feelings, and imagination. Now it cannot even trust a thing it physically experiences again and again. Doubt has cut it off completely from life.

If today the Self comes across a fairy or an angel who granted it a wish on condition that it just has just a moment to ask, do you know what will happen? The Self will lose the chance. It will have to think for the rest of its life what to ask for. Even if it did ask for something, that will not be the true wish of its heart, but from the mind. The Self, out of greed, will ask for something like the Midas Touch that will turn everything into gold, not realizing the wish will cause more misery in life than joy.

In this disconnected state of the heart, how can the Self expect to live a life of joy? When it cannot trust its own heart, is not trusting life a far cry? To wish and imagine with the heart has become impossible for the Self. Imagination is now a prisoner of fear and doubt. Expectation is completely negative. Life energies and the mind are engaged day and night in finding an invulnerable shield against dangers which the Self constantly imagines. Where is the freedom to live? How will the Self trust and abandon to the Ocean of the Supreme Reality? Freedom will come when the Self sees its present reality. So we must see in depth how the heart destroys its own freedom and then itself.

Today what the Self thinks is its heart is actually the mind. The Self's urges now are urges of the mind only. They arise from psychological compulsions and material needs only. A true heart never thinks what it wants -- it feels it. It is always aware of its true seeking. The reason the Self has to think what it wants is that the mind is insecure and wants too many things. Doubt and greed do not let it choose. In fact the true wish of the Self today is -- to know the true wish of its heart. This is the wish the Self should ask for if it comes across a fairy. Once the Self begins living from its heart again, feelings will revive; the Self will be able to feel its heart deeper and know the forgotten true quest.

Experiencing the Supreme Reality is the original quest of the Self that it has forgotten about. Reunion with the Supreme Being is the hidden true wish of the heart. The Self has been separated from its Infinite Source for eons now. Till the Self feels its heart very deeply, it will not remember it. Its present attachments are only with the material. It does not accept anything else. In the transitory material world, its identity comes from thoughts and emotions about its image, body, and possessions. Deep inside, the Self is in constant fear that these things will end one day. Only knowing the Truth will free the Self. Once the mind gets out of the way, the heart will take over life again. Then the Self can live from the heart like a child, know what it truly loves, and begin seeking it.

Modern society wants human beings to live mechanically and perform like highly efficient machines without any Self-choices. Tasks are assigned from outside and motivation is fed from outside. How to live, how to love, how to have faith, how to be happy, how to be sad, how to pray, how to have sex, how to eat, how to sleep, how to find a friend, how to find a marriage partner, how to bring up children ... human life now is driven by HOW TOs. The Self is living within a groove made for it by society. It is merely doing what is expected of it. How well it conforms determines how well it has performed. The Self is praised and rewarded when it follows rules set by others for it. The Self has been conditioned even about when to feel happy and sad. Where is the true Self? Where is the heart? Where are its choices? Where is happiness? Where is the quest for Supreme Reality? The wonderful results we have achieved in the name of modernity, rationality and science are in front of us. Let us see our Report Card: a plundered planet that very soon will not be able to sustain us, a world full of religious and political conflict, violence and insanity as a means of pleasure, dysfunctional families, religions that give no peace and path, science that is itself confused, monetary systems choked by greed, love that does not last more than a moment, faith that is running for cover from fear ... the list is endless. I have to stop somewhere, otherwise this book will only be filled with destruction caused by heartless living. We have become adept at designing problems and then researching for solutions. Between these dynamics we get a sense of control, rational living, achievement, and pride. We are merely feeding our minds and growing them larger. But remember: the larger the mind, the more its doubt, fear, and confusion.

The heart has suffered since the beginning in this world. No one has felt its pain and loneliness. No one has felt its wounds. It has been crying for freedom and true expression all through eternity. Its voice has always been smothered -- sometimes for approval, at other times to honor the mores of society. The heart has been brutalized whenever it has been expressed truly in a Messiah, in a Mystic, in an innocent lover, in a compassionate reformer, in an inventor, in an explorer, in a scientist -- let alone in the common man. No one takes sides with the heart, not even the Self it belongs to. When the Self does not listen to its own heart, no one else will. From prehistoric to modern times, the heart has always remained in the bondage of society. Apparently the individual has more voice today, but where is free will? Society still rules the individual through its material needs. Physical force was used in the past; now cunning reasoning is used to convince and manipulate. Society sells you what it wants to sell. As long as the source of happiness is not from within the heart, false pleasure and greed will exist, and there will be no freedom. The "How to do it" bondage I mentioned earlier is the way society controls the individual today. As long there is ignorance of Truth, this slavery will not end. The heart will not become free. Without the heart, the Supreme Being cannot be sought.

There was a time when at least during early childhood the heart used to be the center of living. Not now. The poison of attachment with the false has sent its roots right up to the beginning of human life on earth. Today a child is barely out of the cradle when the world begins conditioning it, away from innocence, into a totally heartless being. Pressure to perform, and not instincts, shape a human being now. Parents feel great when their child begins thinking and behaving as a grownup very early. How is this progress? Now we begin expressing unhappiness, disinterest, and conflict even in early childhood.

The heart is the true Self's voice. How will you live without it? You are rooted into life through it. The first thing that mankind urgently needs today is HEALING. The Self needs healing, society needs healing, the world needs healing. But there will be no lasting healing until the heart is healed. Healing the heart means freeing it from repression due to ignorance of the mind. A measure of unhappiness of the heart can be had from the expression of the blocked vital forces, as countless dreaded diseases like cancers, arterial hardening and blocks, Alzheimer's, Parkinson's, Attention Deficient Disorders, etc. The mental, emotional, and physical spheres of the Self have fallen apart. The ability to feel from the heart has become dead. Nothing is interesting to the Self for long. From this inner turmoil and discontent, the Self is continuing to destroy itself and its environment.

The Self has not lived from its own heart for many lives. The Self fears it and does not trust it now. The Self has become used to indirect happiness -- a happiness that is dependent upon approval of others. Because the Self represses its voice, it does not feel free. It blames others for this lack of freedom. The repressed urges seek sudden, varied, and violent fulfillment. The Self conforms in order to win praise from others all the time. The Self is choked. It now expresses freedom in perversion, both sadistic and masochistic. The Self has to discover its true heart hidden beneath a mountain of lies, fears, insecurities, anxieties, greed, futile struggles, and misunderstandings. It has been drifting away from its heart for several lifetimes. The mind caused this. It all began when Self-image became more important to the Self than the true and innocent feelings of its heart. On one hand, the Self was becoming a freer individual; on the other hand its happiness was becoming dependent on approval of others. So it fell into a deeper bondage. The Self's choices became dependent on others again. The Self's true happiness dried up.

How to revive the heart?

To revive the heart the Supreme Reality has to be revealed to the Self. Such is the power of revelation about the Supreme Being that all pain and misery vanish. The original desire is felt again. Love, faith, courage, and feelings begin reviving. The Self becomes free of repressions, inner conflict, and material attachments.

Where does the Self get this Truth from? Religion is playing a very irresponsible role in freeing the Self and society. It is not answering what it is supposed to be answering. Religion arose in this world to show the way to the Self toward Ultimate Freedom. All religions originated from Prophets, Saints, and Mystics who taught love, living from the heart, and tolerance. But religion has interpreted these teachings very differently. So a big part of human energy is taken up by battling with problems caused by conflict between Self and religion, and between different religions. To fight over the Supreme Being is the ultimate desecration of The Truth. If such practices earn heaven, this conflict will continue in heaven too. If such perceptions about Truth are rewarded by the Supreme Being, such a being cannot be supreme. What the Self has failed to understand, ever since the beginning of time, is that there can be infinite viewpoints toward the Supreme Being and infinite paths to become one with it. When Supreme Truth is one, why waste energy in conflicts over which path is superior? Mankind has to come out its ignorant reasoning and savage justice. Otherwise we are no different from the era of nailing at the cross and burning at the stake. The Supreme Being is one. All religions give a path toward the same destination. Just follow the one your heart likes, and you will arrive.

Receive Truth from a real source where it is happening today. Truth is a very inductive thing. Its qualities are very magnetic. It can jump like a flame. It can revive the heart and brighten your life, like one lamp lights another. Some revelation, some expression, some demonstration given by a being living from the Truth could open your heart to this vast realm. You will drop all resistance of the mind during such a moment.

Finding the heart is essential to seek the Supreme Being. The heart is the source of love and faith without which the Self cannot have the pure senses, dedicated attention, and endless perseverance required on the path. See how a honey bee can find a blooming flower, miles away? The bee is seeking nectar. Its entire life energy is focused toward it.

Find your heart first.

8

Faith

*Without faith, the Self can never experience the
Supreme Being.
Relating with the unknown and formless requires
ultimate faith. The heart has this capacity. Know
about the Supreme Being and live from faith to
find deeper faith. When faith becomes total, the
Ultimate experience will happen.*

Faith is accepting the Supreme Being before experiencing.
Faith is accepting something that is beyond the grasp of the
mind. Faith is accepting something before experiencing it.
The Self can never experience what it does not have faith
in. Faith precedes experience.

Why is faith essential?

The Source of the Self is infinite. Life exists within
an infinite unknown. The Self arose from this unknown
and is rooted in it, whether it accepts this or not. Life
happens constantly at the junction of unknown and known.

Experience is constantly a step into the unknown from the known. And by this process the Self evolves its consciousness. The unknown scares the human mind. The mind wishes for complete control over the unknown. It wishes to find complete security against the unknown. In order to achieve that, it wishes to arrive at an ultimate understanding and conclusion about it. Religion and science answer this core need of the human mind. They make the Self feel in control. Science controls the known; Religion the unknown. But life is too mighty and unlimited. It occasionally breaks through human armor with something new and more powerful. Such a challenge unsettles existing beliefs by exposing them. Again the Self begins a new pursuit to find an invincible fortification. Someday the Self has to understand that Faith in the Supreme Being is the only faith that can answer this core need. Scientific knowledge and guesses about the unknown will never free the Self of fear. The Self has to experience the Supreme Being, and know the True Reality, in order to end all doubt and find absolute security.

To experience the Supreme Being, the Self has to have faith in the Supreme Being. The Self has to accept the Supreme Reality and begin living from it. When the Self experiences its Spiritual Truth, all doubt will dissolve.

Why can the Self not trust the Supreme Reality?

Every day you trust thousands of things you do not know about, or which you know little about. In many situations, your life is at risk. You trust the plane and the pilot when you fly; you trust the trains and buses, and their drivers, when you travel on land; you trust your car, your skills, and those of other drivers when you drive; you trust your doctor, the procedures, and the medicines; you trust your equipment when you go parachuting, scuba diving, river rafting, or mountaineering. The list of what you trust without knowing much about it, and having no control, is endless. Many disasters happen which expose the limits up to which human mind and science can foresee. Yet your faith in them never wavers for long. You protect your faith by reasoning that the accident was an exception and a low probability event. If the Self can trust all these things, why can it not trust the Supreme Being, and become free of fear forever? Why the Self cannot trust the Supreme Being is because the Supreme Reality cannot be grasped by the mind. It is a total unknown for the Self. The Self has no clue about it. The Self can never control it. The mind dislikes a situation it cannot control, either today, or someday in the future.

As a child we could trust because there was no mind. There was no past. There was no knowledge. The future could not be projected from any past of the Self. The future was pure imagination. The "I" had not formed yet. There was nothing to be protected. There was desire, but it was pure. It was not to protect an "I." Pure desire does not cause any fear. That is why there was trust. Imagination could be trusted.

Never forget one truth: nothing in life is risk free other than The Supreme Truth. So, know about the Supreme Being, find faith, and seek the Supreme Being. Do not waste life in waiting for a time when a disaster will prove the fragility of beliefs of the mind.

The other thing is you are here to experience the reality of the Self. Arriving at it is Supreme joy. Any phenomenon experienced through total faith is very different than that which you experience through the mind. The experience through fully developed faith is not past-dependent.

Without faith, the Supreme Being cannot be experienced. True Reality is not on a continuum with the processes of knowing of the mind. The mind can never arrive there. Faith is the only bridge available to the Self for the crossover into Supreme Reality. What a wonderful power faith is! It connects the Known with the Unknown: it begins in the Known and ends in the Unknown.

Live from faith, so that it becomes unwavering. Faith has to hold when life tests. And life will constantly test it. It requires courage and persistent hard work. The Self has to make itself vulnerable to Creation and life. How else will the Self ever know who is truly running its life? It requires knowing, reasoning, patience, self-control, effort, and surrender. Fear and doubt are the nature of the mind. They will oppose faith. Knowing about the Supreme Reality will dissolve them. Once the Self experiences The Truth in real life, the Self will begin to become free of the mind, and faith will begin holding.

Prayer helps to find faith. First the Self prays to ask for protection against harm, and for realization of its material wishes. The prayer is answered, and faith develops. A seeker prays for an experience of the Supreme Reality and for unwavering faith when life tests. The prayer is answered, and faith becomes stronger. A Prophet, Messiah, a Saint prays and asks for more awareness in the world and peace and happiness for mankind. They ask for Divine help and ultimate faith to live through ultimate situations. The prayer is answered and ultimate faith and its power is demonstrated. Life continues to purify the Self toward eventual oneness with the Supreme Reality, whether the Self has faith or not. The processes of Creation are independent of what the mind wants. Pain and misery will be there. Death and destruction will be there. Nothing can be avoided. Every experience, pleasant and unpleasant, is required. Never forget that even those who are consciously not on the path are also on the same path. This is the Ultimate Truth.

A truth which is experienced deep within your

subjectivity only, secluded in mountains, in forests, away from relationships and society, may not hold when life tests. It could be an imagined state also. The mind could fool the Self. In real life it cannot. Life is the touchstone of Faith. Prophets, Saints, and Mystics lived as normal human beings, and their Truth was tested by life. Life is the touchstone that passes only 24 karat gold. No impurities are allowed. There is no exemption for anyone.

The true touchstone of every path is that it should work, and give a result: a result that is felt as joy and freedom by your heart. If you have found one that is working, it clears this touchstone test. Never try to confirm what is already working by comparing it with something else. This will cause mis-faith.

Only total faith opens the door to the Supreme Being and true living.

9

Reason

Reason is the ultimate faculty; it frees the Self from the mind in order to experience the Supreme Being.

Reason is the inherent and highest power of the Self by which it can become free from the mind. Pure reason is from the Supreme Truth. Pure reason stands on truths of Creation and life. Pure reason stands on true facts of life. Pure reason frees love from the attachments of the mind. Pure reason frees faith from fear and doubt, and makes it total. Pure reason frees the Self toward experiencing the Supreme Being. Reason is always toward an objective. The higher the objective of the reason, the truer the reason. When the objective is to reveal the Ultimate Truth to a mind by reason, reason has to be at its purest level.

Only Masters have pure reason. They can reason from the Supreme Truth to free the Self from the mind and awaken it. Such reason flows directly from the Supreme Being in the moment. It is most powerful and has the potential to cause spontaneous enlightenment in an advanced seeker. It is crystal clear like a diamond and can cut across the hardest ignorance of the mind.

The mind of a seeker should never form conclusions until the Self arrives at the Supreme Reality. To do this, a higher reason has to constantly free the mind from a lower reason. The mind has a tendency to conclude because it does not exist in non-conclusion. It goes silent. It dissolves. A Master's reason is unlimited. Masters do not reason from a conclusion. Their reason is free. They can reason for and against in a situation from The Truth. Their objective is not to win a point, but to free the Self from the mind. Reason is a device for them. Their reason constantly evolves.

Love, Faith, and Reason are the three ultimate qualities of the Supreme Being. They are the three legs on which Supreme Reality stands in Creation. Each one of them is dependent on the other two. They can be experienced separately in Creation, but in the Supreme Reality they are in complete oneness. In a seeker all of them have to be developed and integrated. In every path, one of them is dominant at the beginning. Masters use them according to their experiences, and depending upon the state of seekers they work with.

The entire Universe is organized on reason, is controlled by reason. Galaxies, black holes, solar systems, planets ... everything down to a grain of sand is reason-dependent for its existence. The human mind and human body cannot exist and function without reason.

Reason is such a powerful and essential faculty in human beings that nothing can work without it. Life is unimaginable without it. It is used in every domain of life. Every human feeling, thought, and emotion depends upon some reason. Religion and Science cannot operate without it. We cannot evolve without it. Reason reveals the Know

Why of things. It gives us the Why of everything. It is the most powerful faculty of the human mind. Every human being uses it in every moment to make choices.

But reason is double-edged. It can free the Self from bondage of the mind as well create bondage of the mind. True reason liberates the mind. Blind reason causes deeper ignorance. Blind reason is caused by ignorance of True Reality. It causes illusions, compulsions, and fears of the mind. Blind reason becomes deepest bondage when it causes blind faith. This is the bondage religions have to become free from. This is the bondage Prophets, Saints, and Mystics worked against. It is the main cause of misery, pain, and conflict in the world.

Until the Self lives, it will have to use reason to keep itself free from doubt and fear. Prophets, Saints, and Mystics used it till their last breath. Awakened Love is the supreme reason.

True reason should be made the touchstone for every thought, emotion, and act on the path.

10

Mind

The Self's "I" consciousness comes from the mind. The Self thinks it is the mind. The Self has to become free from it to become one with the Supreme Being.

The mind is the individuality of the Self. It keeps a unique quality of the Supreme Being separate from it. It is a personal space created and enclosed by thought. Its center is the "I" of the Self. It is a temporary state within The Whole. It is a home for the Self during its journey through life.

The human mind has three basic forms: a non-seeker's mind is totally closed like a sphere; a seeker's mind is open at the top and is like a hemisphere; an enlightened being's mind is open at both ends and is like a hollow reed. At the beginning the mind has to be closed. At this stage the mind is like an eggshell. The Self is yet in a stage of development and maturation. It is the embryonic stage of the Self. When the Self becomes a seeker the mind has to gradually open. The Truth cannot be received otherwise. A seeker's mind becomes hemispherical -- open at the top. It is like a vessel, the begging bowl of ascetics. The Self in this stage has to gather Truth about the Supreme Being. It requires total acceptance and humility. The ultimate shape of the mind is a hollow reed having an infinite aperture. Such a mind is completely passive. It can retain nothing. It can add nothing. As the Divine content passes through it, the Divine tune is heard.

Creation began when the "I" felt separate from the Supreme Consciousness. A center of consciousness that felt separate from the rest was formed. It caused a mind. It created space and distance. The "I" felt an enclosed space that had boundaries. The "I" felt the urge for knowing and experiencing. The individual consciousness began experiencing the reality outside of itself. It being unique, its experiences were unique. The "I" consciousness began feeling love for itself. It became attached to itself. It began forgetting the Original Reality. Gradually it came to feel that it is the doer. It began owning its qualities. It began feeling pride in them. This gave it happiness. It wanted a repetition of experiences. It began remembering experiences. The dual nature of Creation also caused opposites. The need for choice arose. The shell around the "I" kept becoming more defined. It became a memory of all its past experiences, which began influencing all later experiences.

First to arise was the Divine "I" and the Divine mind. It is the mind of Creation. It is the original feeling of Self-consciousness that formed within the Supreme Consciousness. It is all the universal laws that control Creation and organized life. In the reality beyond Creation, the Supreme Being has no center and no boundaries. It is open-ended. It is formless. It is oneness. It is opposites together. There is no separation. There is no distance. There is no motive. There is no movement. There is no beginning. There is no end. There is no mind. But Creation arose when an infinite "I" arose, created space and distance, and began evolving Reality. Initially there was only this Divine "I" and universal processes. Gradually the infinite processes began dividing into smaller and smaller expressions. The laws of Creation being universal, what is true for the microcosm is also true for the macrocosm. The universe, galaxies, constellations, stars, solar systems, planets, oceans, mountains -- all forms of life, right up to atomic and subatomic levels, developed within their own shells. The human mind is a shell. The human womb is a shell. An egg is a shell. A seed is a shell. An atom is a shell. A nucleus is a shell. We can go on and on. Shells exist within shells. Otherwise, creative processes cannot operate. Shells separate qualities and enclose them. Creative laws give them form and regulate them. Polarities balance them. And love motivates and relates all processes within the grand overall shell of Creation. This is the story of genesis of the mind.

The Reality of the "I" and the mind has been seen as illusory by Saints and Mystics to indicate to the Self that there is a vaster Reality beyond, and that phenomenal reality is fragmentary and relative. In this reality the Self thinks, as well as feels, that it is separate from everything else in Creation.

The Self thinks the extent of its Self is its body, feelings, and thoughts. This it sees as its identity. The Self loves and wants to protect and grow this sense of "I." It does not want any harm to come to it. It wishes it to exist forever. It is attached to it. It feels pride in it. It wishes it to be the best out of all around. If any experience endangers it, the Self feels fearful. If any experience denies its understanding, the Self feels hurt. The Self seeks only experiences favorable toward its "I." This is the Self's present happiness. Life has become a constant pursuit toward these desires of the mind.

From the unawakened state, the Self thinks freedom is just being able to do what it wants or being able to remain free of what it does not want. As long as life is fulfilling the Self's wishes, it sees it as good luck and is happy. But the slightest opposition to a wish destroys this fragile happiness and feeling of freedom. This is the nature of the ignorant mind. This is its turmoil.

The knowing with the mind is relative and does not hold. The Self wants it to work forever, but it does not. It is inconsistent. You see a ray of light in one direction and go that way. Everything works for you for a while; then it ceases, and you are back in confusion. Then you go the other way and the same happens. This is the constant movement of the mind.

In the realm of the mind, the Self's beliefs about the Supreme Reality are no better. They have been handed down from the past. They are not rooted in the Reality of present life. Now if this is the quality of life you wish to continue living, suffering and uncertainty will remain a part of it.

The "I" Self cannot even feel true love. It is scared to let go in love also. The "I" sees love also as loss of control. This is the same uneasiness the mind feels in true happiness, because "I" begins dissolving in it, and that scares it. The mind seeks a happiness it can control. When the Self is seeking happiness, it is actually seeking the security of its known and existing structures, a repetition of past experiences which felt pleasant to the "I," not an experience with the real.

The Self prefers the familiar and avoids the unknown. Day breaks, night falls; the Self is mechanically doing the same acts in the same way day after day. The Self continues to exist inattentively. Only when life challenges it in a new manner against its wishes, it forces the Self to be attentive. The Self has no deep contentment at every sunset of having lived a day well. And there is no eagerness and looking forward to another day for doing what the heart wishes. There is no waking up excited every morning like a child to explore and experience the new.

The constant fear of the "I" Self is that something unknown might challenge it … something it might not be able to handle. So its constant attempt is to tame nature and the unknown. The ultimate fear is that the "I" will one day cease to exist. This the Self sees as its end. That is why it fears the unknown. Death is the greatest unknown it has no control over. The "I" has imagined God to be a Supreme Power, and has formed many beliefs to ensure it will live after death. Since the "I" can relate to, understand, possess, and control only forms, it imagines God in some form and gives God qualities that can protect it.

The Self's wish is to continue sleeping within its illusory reality. The dreams are very pleasant for it. What has the false reality given to the Self? It is always scared even after so much fortification around. It is lonely even after relating with so many. It is suspicious of even those it loves, and opposes true nearness to them. It is uncertain even after acquiring so much knowledge. It is tired and bored even with things it so fondly sought once. It is being thrashed in a whirlpool of thoughts day and night. Its image conflicts what its heart wishes.

But the Self is not learning its lessons. It is misusing the creative energies made available to it for experiencing its True Reality. It is opposing Creation and life with the power available to it. Its increasing disorder is the proof. It is like a fish attempting to learn to live outside water.

The foolishness is that it thinks it will find happiness in this un-naturalness. Benevolent Creation will never let it happen; otherwise the Self would never be able to become free from this false world of the mind and thoughts.

Acceptance and a deep transformation are required, because the Self loves its bondage. There is a tale of the mermaid who fell in love with a sailor. To live alongside him on land she asked for a wish, that her tail would be changed into human legs. Her wish was granted on a condition: her every step would feel as if she were walking on sharp swords and live coals. The Self's suffering due to living outside the True Reality is no less than the mermaid's. The Self is separated from its source, the Supreme Being. The Self has become mind-centered. It is attached to a false Reality and its pleasures. The Self is also like a fish out of water. It is gasping for life in this unnatural environment, but does not want to let it go.

Creation allows the Self complete freedom of Will. But its laws do not relax for anyone. What the Self sows today it will have to reap in the future. It cannot cry then. It should not see life as harsh and unfair when it has to face its doings. Pain and suffering will never end in the domain of mind centered "I" and its illusory Reality. Freedom does not exist in these attachments. The possibility of seeking the Real exists only beyond this acceptance. The Self is scared of True Reality because it thinks it would lose its present "I" in it. It wishes this "I" to survive while also finding The Ultimate Reality. This cannot happen.

The mind does not let the Self see True Reality. That is why the spiritual viewpoint sees it as the block, and recommends dropping it. But life is not possible without a mind. The mind cannot be dropped, but has to transform. It has to become true. A true mind is the mind of a seeker. It is open at the top like a vessel and accepts the Supreme

Reality. An awakened mind is a mind that has experienced the Supreme Being. It has become open at both ends. It is what has been called "the hollow reed" by Masters. It is passive and is expressing the Supreme Being. Only the Masters understand all states of the mind and its power. They also know how to guide the mind of a seeker on the path in the right way for result.

To become free from the mind, we do not have to overcome it. We have to know it. We have to understand it. After all, the constraints we now need to shed were essential once. This moment stands upon countless previous moments. Countless experiences of the past gradually opened up the consciousness of the Self. The whole process has to be understood to achieve freedom. The mind is a vessel that contains life. It is essential. Life is conceived within the mind. It grows within the mind. But one day the hard shell becomes the barrier to ultimate experiencing. Life now wants to reach out for the heavens. It wishes to experience ultimate beauties and potentials. It wishes to experience infinite acts. It wishes to experience the magnificence of its source. It wishes to merge with it, like a river falling into the sea. To experience the Supreme Reality, the mind has to pass through a metamorphosis. It has to develop open dimensions, and become totally open at the top. It has to become like a bowl that has collected several drops, but is constantly open to raindrops. It has to become like the soil to a tree. It gives nourishment and support to the roots, but the branches have freedom to grow outwards. The problem arises when the mind attempts to define the sky or fear skyward growth.

What will cause this transformation?

Revelation about the Supreme Reality to the mind will initiate it. The mind has an essential nature. It wants the ultimate. It wants bliss. It wants to know the ultimate. It is open to reason -- especially to reason from True Reality and experienced facts. The core urge of the mind is to come to rest at an acceptable truth. It is tired from a long journey. But it will surrender only when it comes across something far more beautiful than it has ever imagined, and its fears are clarified. So the first thing is that the revealed Truth has to be acceptable to the heart as well reasonable to the mind. If brought face to face with such a Truth the mind will find it irresistible. It will take it in and then surrender. Awakening to Reality will cause the past to become silent. The Limited will cease; the Unlimited will arise. The Self has to die to the past to be reborn in the present.

Do not worry about how you will live without conscious control of the mind after the Self surrenders to the Supreme Reality. Creation loves the Self and will handle it with great care. Have Faith and try. Once you experience it, the mind will come to rest and become silent. Uncaused miracles will begin happening in life. Till now, the Self struggled to cause them. Natural processes will begin operating, and true flow will revive. All wounds and pains of the Self will heal. The Self's only contribution in the new and joyous Reality is that Faith has to be found and maintained. Never ever mistrust and ask what will come next -- this will stop the experience immediately. Here you will require all your Faith in the Supreme Being. Greed for a heaven will also not let the door open or the miracles happen. The Self has to be total in every moment and it must allow, passively and silently. The least effort or thought destroys the experience of Reality. The Self cannot even struggle with its mind. The passivity must be this extreme.

The mind of a seeker becomes open with Faith, and keeps becoming more open with experiences of True Reality. A mind is required in Creation, but the Self has to awaken to the fact that it is not just the mind. It is much more than that. Only human consciousness has the potential to experience the Supreme Reality. A True Mind is the vessel for receiving the Supreme Reality.

There are some traits of the mind that are barriers to experiencing the Supreme Being. Working on them will free the mind to trueness. Once the mind becomes free and passive it is ready to receive Reality. The trait of the mind that has to be especially watched is PRIDE. Pride is the main block that does not let the Self merge with The Infinite Source. All Masters lay great stress on practicing humility to become free from it.

The seeker will have to be very cautious of pride. Its old structures will have to be dismantled. Its new and subtle structures have to be guarded against. Pride is the dearest thing to the "I." Love for the "I" causes it. It is most difficult to free the mind from it. Even beyond enlightenment, it has to be watched. Such is the grip of pride on the Self that even when life is constantly indicating through misery, pain, reversals, losses, insults, and ill-health that it is the cause of pain, the Self does not easily accept that Pride is the cause. It is the ultimate block to experiencing the Supreme Reality. It closes the mind and blinds the senses. It causes anger, a diseased sensitivity, and hyperreaction in the Self. It makes the Self look down on everything. The Self is attentive only to its own "I." It makes the Self's attention deficient toward life and surroundings. It kills all interest in life, since everything is lesser in appeal to the Self than the "I." In spite of struggling to feel important all the time, the Self lacks self-esteem and genuine happiness. If the Self persists with pride, life has to use humiliation to make the Self aware of it. The first step toward freedom from pride is seeing and accepting it, then remaining observant all the time to free the Self gradually from it. It is difficult to catch it on your own. It can hide behind false humility, religious surrender, and spiritual practices. I have experienced it up to the ultimate. I have experienced its humiliation. I have experienced its cunning. I have experienced its burdens. I have experienced its confusion. I have experienced the destruction it causes. There is no greater poison. Nothing blinds more completely. Becoming free from pride is the main challenge of a seeker.

The other trait that must be seen clearly in order for the mind to free itself is that the mind can exist only in a state and evolves through compensation. For instance, if a Self feels it was cruel at one time, guilt of the mind compensates it with compassion. These compensations go on within one life and from life to life. The Supreme Being is not a state. An advanced seeker has to merge opposite states and move onto pure responses.

Truth can be received only by an empty mind, a still mind, a non-interfering mind ... a mind that is completely free from the past; a mind that lets the heart feel. Because it is only the heart which can feel it has arrived at its Truth. To free the mind, reason your way out of the bondage. You have to detach from what you know and seek the True Reality with a fresh mind and heart like a child's. Even a whiff of Truth is out of the question till mind is free and crystal clear. The true childlike seeker has to emerge.

The Self cannot experience true freedom until it becomes free from its own "I" and its ignorance about Reality.

11

Desire

*The core desire of the Self is to experience the
Supreme Being. Without desire, the Supreme
Being cannot be experienced.*

Desire is the urge to experience something. Desire is love
focused on something. The object is experience. Desire
is attached love. Desire is a want of the Self, in its state
of separation from the Supreme Being. It is the wish for
something which the Self feels would make it complete and
happy. Desire ends in oneness with what is desired. That is
why everything ends in merging with the Supreme Being.
There is no desire in absolute oneness.

Desire created the Self. Desire evolves the Self. Desire
creates bondage for the Self. Desire frees the Self. The
original desire of the Self is to experience the Supreme
Reality. When the Self experiences the Supreme Being, it
will be fulfilled.

The instruments of the Self to feel a desire and experience
what is desired are the senses. Experiencing something

from outside is with outer senses. Experiencing something from outside passes through the physical and the mind. It is with outer physical senses and inner conditioned senses of the mind. Pure experiencing is innermost experiencing and is very different. The Self becomes one with what has to be experienced. Experiencing something by being one with it is through the deepest inner senses. When you feel a desire within your heart, you use the inner senses. You begin to become one with it. Once oneness is total, there is no desire and no experience. The experiencer merges with the experienced. The experience with the Supreme Being extends across the entire bandwidth. It is an outer and an inner experience, and then, complete oneness.

The Self is fragmented into several desires. Every moment the senses pick up something, the Self begins desiring. This process is endless. In the world, the new and more beautiful constantly appears. The Self exists in a state of unfulfilled desires constantly. This keeps the Self unhappy. This keeps the Self in misery and pain. Does that mean we stop desiring? But even the desire to stop desiring is, itself, a desire. So what is the true way?

The "I" Self can never answer all its desires. The mind by its very nature can never be complete. The mind is a device that was caused by desire and it can exist only while there is desire. So the Self moves from one desire to another in search of lasting peace and happiness. This is the desire of the Self which has remained elusive. It can never be fulfilled until the Self discovers its true desire into which all other desires merge.

Desire is attached and focused energy of love. It is the most powerful thing. It is double-edged. It can be used in either direction: it can free the Self, or create more bondage. It can take the Self toward reality, and also toward ignorance. The power of desire has to be used with awareness in order to become free. Anything can be done with desire. An ignorant Self is ruled by desire. A seeker becomes free through desire. A seeker is in control of desire and does not let the mind scatter into countless desires. Masters recommend a state of desirelessness to seekers. It is essential for freeing and silencing the mind, in order to experience the Supreme Being. But it has different meanings on different paths and at different stages of seeking. The Self's consciousness is scattered into many desires. These must be gathered into a single desire. All the love of the Self has to build up one desire. It has to come to focus in one desire.

All desires cause fear. The fear of the Self is what will happen if its desire is not fulfilled. The fear is of harm to what the Self loves. The fear is for the security of the "I," its understanding and emotions. The fear is of emotional hurt. This causes negative expectation and the Self loses faith in itself and life. There is only one desire in Creation that causes the fear which desires surrender and dissolution. It is the only fear that grows faith and frees the Self: the desire for the Supreme Being. The nature of this supreme desire is very different. It is not to protect the core illusion of the Self -- the "I." It is to dissolve it. It is the only desire where result is certain. Because when you desire the Supreme Being it is certain the desire will be fulfilled, a meeting will happen; there is no question of fulfillment. The Self fears only whether the path is right or not.

On the path of love, gather all desires into one desire: desire for the Supreme Being. Once the Self experiences the Supreme Being it becomes truly desire-less.

12

Surrender

The Supreme Reality is across surrender of the "I," its attachments, and its possessions.

Surrender is letting go. Surrender is abandoning. True Surrender is essential for oneness with the Supreme Being. For a seeker, it is letting go of what you are attached to the most. It is beginning to live from complete faith in the Supreme Being, Creation, and life. It can happen only when the Self has gone to the very extreme pursuing something in life, and still has not found peace and happiness.

Surrender is unique and very beautiful on the path of love toward the Supreme Being. It is from the heart and a desire. It is not a compulsion. There is joy in this surrender. As the Self surrenders what is dearest to it, it feels a rare joy. A Self in love is never satisfied with extent of surrender, and wants to surrender more and more. Only through surrender can love be felt. The Self is even prepared to die for its love. Ultimate joy is in surrendering till nothing remains. Ultimate joy is ecstasy.

Life ripens the Self by passing it through many experiences of pleasure, pain, and misery; through experiences that build the Self's pride, and experiences that humiliate it. The Self constantly struggles against what it does not want. This keeps it always in turmoil. From the poorest to the richest, every human being has some incompleteness they are vainly fighting against. There is no freedom, no relief; because there is no acceptance of Reality, and there is no surrender to it.

The might of life humbles every being sooner or later. If the Self does not awaken with such experiences, the pain causes permanent wounds. The Self tries to hide and compensate for such states. The scars are carried life after life. They shape the makeup of the Self in future lives. These unpleasant experiences give weaknesses and fears to the Self. Only surrender can heal these wounds.

Every Self pursues something in the material world above everything else. Every Self has something closest to its heart. Every Self gathers more and more of it to satisfy this desire. The pursuit gives happiness. It gives the Self a purpose and hope of becoming complete. This process matures the Self for the Supreme Reality. This creates an opportunity for acceptance and awakening to the Truth someday. It also gives the Self something to surrender as a price for experiencing the Supreme Reality. It is from this bank account the Self spends when it becomes a seeker. These are the dynamics of life to mature a seeker.

A Self ripe for surrender is highly crystallized and hardened. Its loves are defined. Above everything else, it loves itself -- its "I," mind, and body. Its reasoning, right or wrong, is unbending. It has deep beliefs and convictions. It has gathered a very big "I," -- an "I" that it does not wish to surrender at any cost. It is defending its "I" with all its resources. Arriving at this state of the "I" is essential for the surrender to Supreme Reality.

How surrender develops is as follows. The Self has core needs: the need for security, the need to feel complete and happy. All other needs and pursuits in life arise from these core needs. The Self seeks a way of life that gives these. It seeks power over all forces of life to acquire these needs. The Self chooses some way of living, some pursuit, that seems to answer these needs. It works for a time. It gives results. The Self feels happy. The Self keeps on travelling toward the very extreme of the chosen pursuit, to arrive at absolute security and completeness. As long nothing unsettles the Self, this is a perfect world. The Self loves it and trusts it. The Self protects it. Complacency develops as confidence grows. But life keeps on posing larger and larger questions. One day an event exposes the illusory reality. The Self's reality shows vulnerability. A Self which has gone to the extreme has nowhere further to go. This experience is miserable, but causes disillusionment and awakening.

Beyond the disillusionment and awakening, the Self finds its true and final love -- love for the Supreme Being. To experience love, the surrender of what you have gathered is essential. Love can only be experienced beyond surrendering and by surrendering. What will the Self surrender in love with the Supreme Being if it has gathered nothing?

Whatever your love, belief, attachment -- trust it totally, pursue it to the very extreme, and experience its limits ... to ripen for surrender to the Supreme Reality.

13

Fear

The desires and attachments of the "I" cause fear.

Fear is concern about what you want to happen. Fear also is what you do not want to happen to you. The core thing the Self never wants is Not Being. Fear arises from love for the "I." Fear has its source in attachment. The more attached the Self is to something or to a situation, the greater the fear. Desire is a choice of the Self. It is what the Self wants. It is an expectation. The Self does not want a different reality from what it desires. This causes fear.

There is a fear that is pure and beautiful. It is a fear you experience after you become a seeker. It is the fear that arises when you love the Supreme Being. It is a fear that arises not from concern about what will happen to the Self in the unknown domain, but about the eagerness to experience. This fear is: What if I cannot meet the Supreme Being? What if my path is not right?

Life is a waveform. It is undulating. It has peaks and valleys. It has ups and downs. It has good and bad. It has pain and pleasure. This is nature of Creation and life. What we do not want cannot be avoided, if life wants to take us through the experience. Experience would have been half of what it is if there were just one state. There are so many things happening in Creation we do not know about. Knowing about them would also give us fear, but that does not mean we stop knowing. The purpose of life is Self-knowing. The destination of the Self is Ultimate Knowing.

Fear plays a very key role in human evolution. Fear makes the Self seek the Supreme Reality. The Self goes into a sleeping and dreaming state in worldly desires when there is no fear. Fear gives a wakeup call. Fear gives a sense of urgency. Fear makes the Self alert and attentive. It makes the Self single-minded. It makes the senses acute.

Fear in the realm of nature is normal. It exists only in the present. It can only be sensed. It cannot be thought about. Birds and animals also respond against Not-being. But it is a response of life, not of the mind. They have no thought and memory. They cannot imagine death, nor plan to avoid it. The experience of a hostile environment evolves higher skills in them to handle a situation better in the future. It causes a conditioning and DNA mutations, but does not make them generally fearful of life. They do not have an "I" conscious of itself. They do not live outside the existing Reality. They merely seek within it what will meet their need in the moment.

Every living cell in Creation responds against Not-being. But it is only the human Self that thinks fearfully. This is because it has a mind which holds memory of past suffering. It constantly projects an insecure future. The human mind has a sense of "I." The deeper the sense of "I" in the mind, the more fears the Self feels. That is why in a narcissistic state, the mind is paranoid. The other thing is humans can control environment. This they carry too far, and think they can control everything in life. When they do not succeed it causes deeper fear. It causes panic. Human beings can imagine. They can project future reality from the past. To control the future, they do it. But they overlook the logical conclusion that if the present cannot be controlled totally, how can the future be controlled? In the thoughts, fear becomes ungrounded in reality. Now even reasoning out of it becomes difficult. Then human beings hide in thoughts away from life. This way, they think they can avoid encountering the Reality they fear ... a Reality they see as unpleasant. Whatever one does, one is still exposed to laws of Creation and the vast unknowable mystery called life.

Imagination is the most vital function of thinking. It is the womb of reality. Reality is conceived within it and is projected outward to the material levels. Once fear takes control of it, beauty and happiness can no longer be imagined -- fearful images begin actualizing.

More suffering causes more fear. Hope dries up. With it goes faith in everything. The whole of Creation becomes suspect. Life becomes suspect. The Self sees only danger and harm. Constant negative expectation saps all love for life. The Self shuts down its faculty of feeling, in order to avoid sorrow. No longer grounded in life, the Self's fears become illusory. The Self is now terrified of even harmless things. It begins existing in a dark shell, having no love, no feeling, no faith, no light, no hope, no interest, no attention, and only negative expectation.

To become free from fear, the Self has to know the Truth. When you are ignorant about the Supreme Reality, you want to create your own Reality to which you are attached. Creation has its own direction and process that is most beneficial for the individual Self. But the Self wants things to happen in its own way, different from life's design. Only Creation knows the most appropriate way and sequence of events. To the Self, these events and situations appear endangering and cause fear and anxiety. Life's sequence seems random and risky. Sometimes what we require after ten days appears in our life today, and we reject it thinking it is not required or opposing. It gives a feeling of loss of control. But if we have faith in the Supreme Being and life, we do not question whether we will know later why something happened. Creation at times creates unfavorable situations and blocks to move you in the right direction. An awakened Self has known the Supreme Truth, has unwavering faith, remains surrendered, waits to understand the true reason, and is fearless. It respects everything and every experience that Creation brings in life without any choice.

Respect fear. If there is one thing you would want to be thankful for, on the day you arrive at the Supreme Reality, it is fear. You would never have become a seeker without fear. You would never have searched deeper and deeper without the doubt it caused. You could never have felt the original desire without fear. Fear is a part of love. How can you shed it? Know about it -- use it on the path toward the Supreme Being.

Only knowing the Supreme Truth can make the Self fearless.

14

Prayer

Prayer is acceptance of the Supreme Reality and surrender to the power of the Supreme Being.

Prayer is an appeal to the Supreme Being. When the Self prays, it accepts the Supreme Power behind Creation. The Self seeks what it wants directly from it. A true relationship with the Supreme Being begins from prayer. It is the realm of the heart. During prayer, the "I" surrenders. When there is no "I," the help, healing, and guidance of the Supreme Being can reach the Self. Re-learn to pray like a child. No guilt, no doubt, no hesitation -- just pure innocence.

When a Self prays and the prayer is answered, the Self experiences the first proof that the Supreme Being exists. Faith begins developing from there. When situations that you cannot solve with any known power you have are somehow solved through prayer, then faith in the Supreme Power develops.

The Self exists in so much misery and pain because it does not accept the Supreme Power. It thinks knowledge can free it of all problems. But in any time, the challenges faced by mankind have remained far more powerful than existing knowledge. They will remain so. Human beings overlook that in Creation, not just solutions evolve, but challenges also evolve. If the things that threaten the human mind were predictable and fixed, the Self could have grown more knowledgeable and powerful and conquered them. But in life when one level of challenges is answered, the next comes into Reality. Regardless of how much knowledge you accumulate or how much science advances, an infinite part of physical reality will always remain mysterious and beyond control of human beings.

Prayer does not mean becoming passive. The Self, rather, becomes free of fear and can live more. Prayer evolves as the Self evolves. First it asks for miracles. Miracles happen. As faith develops and the Self becomes more aware of The Truth, prayer becomes asking for strength to remain unwavering while living through challenges. Finally, a seeker's prayer is for oneness with the Supreme Reality.

Prayer can be silent also. A mind that has accepted The Supreme Truth and has gone silent is in constant Prayer. You could be a scientist exploring into mysteries of Creation but accepting there is a limit up to which the human mind can go, and accepting inner guidance -- that is also prayer. Prayer just means a relationship with the Supreme Truth.

Prayer requires an innocent mind, in order to be answered. An innocent mind is the heart. Only surrender gives that state of mind. A child's mind has that. A child's mind is innocent. It has total faith. It seeks no proof. It just asks from the heart. It has no doubt. That is why a child's prayer is spontaneously answered. Every Self has to seek such innocence again by accepting the Supreme Reality, and experiencing the Supreme Being.

Can even death be avoided by prayer?

Yes it can be, if faith is total. Such faith comes beyond awakening to True Reality. At this level of being, death is understood and not feared. No Prophet, Saint, or Mystic avoided it. However, they could live as long as they wanted.

When you pray, do not hesitate to ask for what you want. The Supreme Being loves you and is happiest when you ask for a wish. When you have accepted the Supreme Being as the ultimate power, where else will you go if things are not working? So pray to your beloved with full confidence and ask for as much as you want, as many times as you want. It will deepen your love and relationship with the Supreme Being. In fact, when you are in need, go nowhere else but to the Supreme Being.

Religion has given the Self a lot of guilt about asking the Supreme Being for what you want. Become free of it. It is affecting your true relationship with the Supreme Being. This is the point from where you began as a child; do it again. Nothing will revive love, faith, and joyous living faster than prayer.

You only go to the Supreme Being with a prayer when in sorrow. Go in joy also. Ask for a greater joy. In a state of sorrow there is doubt. In a state of joy you are closest to Reality. In a state of joy there is no doubt, and miracles spontaneously happen. Never waste such moments in life.

Without prayer, the Self can never relate to and experience the Supreme Being.

15

Selflessness

*Love causes selflessness, and experiences with
the Supreme Being happen.*

True selflessness cannot be achieved. It happens in love.
Love deeper and deeper toward it, and you will arrive at it.
It will happen. A lover expresses its love for the Supreme
Being through it. It is the most desired state on the path
of love. Complete surrender of everything causes it. This is
the state in which experiences of the Supreme Being begin
happening. Such is the power of selflessness in love -- the
insignificant and powerless Self pulls the infinitely powerful
Supreme Being into an embrace. It is like a drop pulls the
entire ocean toward itself by the power of selfless love. It
is difficult to understand with the mind. It is supreme joy.
Even the word supreme cannot describe it.

Selflessness is the ultimate state of the Self while living.
The Self is, but also it is not. A Selfless Self continues to
be a unique being, but has become one with Creation,
like everything in Nature is. But the expressions of this

selflessness are far more beautiful, since this selflessness is a culmination of consciousness. It happened after willful surrender. This is the hollow reed state that Mystics often mention, through which Creation plays its tune. The "I" has dissolved. The mind has become open at both ends. Awareness has become pure.

The Supreme Being is selfless. Creation is selfless. Nature is selfless. Prophets, Saints, and Mystics were selfless. Gurus are selfless. Legendary lovers were selfless. To become one with the Supreme Being, the Self has to become selfless through love. It is the True Reality of the Self. It is a state of pure consciousness. It happens to a seeker on the path. Only selflessness can merge with selflessness, just as only Gold can merge with Gold. The Supreme Being is selfless so the Self has to become selfless for merging with it.

Only love can cause selflessness. Selflessness is unconditional love. Love is the way to selflessness. It can be seen in the supreme love of a dog for its master. Even when the dog is pushed away, its love remains pure. Even when wounded and in pain or weakened and paralyzed by approaching death, the sight of its master and a call makes it respond by wagging its tail. Life has no parallel to this. If you have never had a pet dog, then have one, to experience such transcendent love and ultimate selflessness. A dog's love or surrender has no motive, but is just a pure quality given to it by Creation. I have had many dogs and experienced it. The other animal which has shown selflessness in relationship with human beings is a horse. This also I have personally experienced. Every seeker has to seek this supreme quality through love before the Supreme Being will reveal itself.

Practicing selflessness as a moral value for guaranteeing a place in heaven is an exalted motive, but is still a motive.

True selflessness never happens this way; nor does the Supreme Being reveal itself. If you learn from a dog and touch the same quality of true surrender for The Supreme Master, no other path is required to be spontaneously blessed with The Ultimate Experience.

I have repeated several times, and repeat once more because it is such a key thing on the path of love: only love and still more love and still more love can make the Self selfless. It is the ultimate method. It makes no difference whether you love The Whole or a part of The Whole, as long it is pure and total. It becomes a path to the same Ultimate.

Selflessness is the highest state of a lover in true love. That is why it is the ultimate path to the Supreme Being.

(My dog Sam gave me a lesson in selflessness while dying.)

16

Death

Dying to one's past is true death.
Without dying to its past, the Self cannot
experience the Supreme Being.

Death is the end of everything we think is our Self. It is the beginning of something totally new. There is death in between lives, and also ultimate death, or Dissolution.

Life is a lesser reality than death. Death is the ultimate reality. Avoiding seeing this fact is to lose the opportunity to live for experiencing the True Reality. We fear it the most. Human beings run away from it by forgetting it all their life. No one has been able to escape it. Emperors, Kings, and Conquerors all fell to it. No one could predict or avoid it.

We cannot experience the Supreme Reality without experiencing true death. It is not the end of life, but the end of the "I." It is the end of separation from the Supreme Being. Prophets, Saints, and Mystics, experienced it while living here. They became free from its fear. They became free of their mind. They became free of their past. They awakened after the experience. They lived their true selves beyond it.

All of us have died so many times. But we still fear death. This is because we have never experienced our own death. Others around us did. They were shocked. In death between lives, only the physical body dies. The mind does not. The mind-consciousness we call the soul returns to a space in Creation befitting the Self's level of awareness of The Truth. After psychological rest, the soul takes birth again in another body and continues with the experiences toward ultimate awakening.

We think we are away from death all our life. But death is the closest thing to us. Even now we are dying every moment and being reborn. We are dying in between breaths all the time. We return to our Supreme Source for this infinitesimally small period in between. Our true vitalization comes from there. It is so brief that we are not aware of it. So when we are living, it is not one continuous life, as we think it is. It is life/death/life/death/life/death/ life/death alternating all the time. This is the pulse. Our heartbeat and breathing also follow this inner rhythm. When our time here ends, we expire for the last time and never inspire again. Mystics use this spiritual knowledge in many of their methods. Paths that work through breath control especially are based on this knowledge.

Some people end their lives because of suffering. That is like dropping out. The whole process has to be repeated in another life in similar circumstances. There is no greater disrespect of the Self, life, and Creation. We have no right to end our life. Such a death never gives peace. Peace is the quality of dissolution. You will not find it across the death you know.

Between us and the Supreme Being stands the fear

of death. But it is not the death we know. Physical death does not make the Self merge with the Supreme Being. Only death of the "I" does. Love dissolves the fear of death. No lover is afraid of death. There is no thought in love. In a thoughtless state there can be no fear and no death. Absolute Peace is available only in true death -- the death of the "I." It is Ultimate Freedom. It is far beyond even bliss. Even bliss is an experience.

We cannot live without true dying and we cannot die without ultimate living. Life and death coexist in Creation, within every process.

(I had just returned after burying my dog Angel when this chapter was revealed.)

17

Dissolution

Absolute oneness with the Supreme Being cannot happen without ultimate dissolution of the "I."

Dissolution is the ultimate merging of the Self into the Supreme Being. It is the falling of the river into the ocean. Nothing much can be said about it. But I will here repeat and give the essence of all that has been revealed earlier.

The "I" is the illusion of the Self about its Reality. It is the Self's consciousness attached with a Self-image. The Self thinks it is a mind and a body. The mind is its entire past. It is its conditioned subjectivity. It has to be dissolved and silenced totally. The Supreme Being is the doer of all acts. This Truth has to be known, accepted, and experienced. Only then will the Self awaken, surrender totally, live from Oneness, and dissolve ultimately. The "I" has to be surrendered by surrendering its choices. All choices of the mind are based upon the past. The Divine Will in the choices of Creation has to be respected and allowed to operate. Without love for the Supreme Being, his surrender is not possible. When there is no support from the past, the "I" cannot survive. This is what scares the Self about seeking the Supreme Reality. So the Self runs away from it. There is one thing about The Truth: when it is, nothing else is. Everything else has to end for it to reveal. The Self is afraid of this. But do not worry -- this fear is natural when you begin. It will dissolve on its own. Energy has to be detached from every thought, emotion, and possession. This will silence the mind. It is true death while living. This is the way to peace and bliss. The last stage of living beyond it is selflessness. This is the expression of the Supreme Being through the uniqueness of the Self. Approval and disapproval, riches and poverty, happiness and unhappiness -- all are the same to a dissolved Self. Many ultimately free beings were sawed, chopped, burnt, and nailed, but they remained peaceful ... such is the Supreme State of Dissolution.

Dissolution is the Ultimate Freedom. Call it Nothingness or Everythingness. It is both together. The mind cannot enter this realm, so no more can be said about it.

Love causes selflessness, and selflessness causes ultimate dissolution.

18

Home

The Supreme Reality is the eternal home of the Self. The Self has journeyed for eons and wishes to return home to true security and happiness.

Home is the place where the Self comes to rest. It is the origin of everything. It is the destination of everything. Oneness with the Supreme Being is the eternal home of the Self. The Self came into Creation from this Oneness and will return to it one day.

Observe birds flying homeward at sunset. It will touch something deep within your heart. Watching the instincts of nature from a deep silence is the most exalted meditation. It can reveal the deepest truths to you in the silent and powerful language of the Supreme Truth.

The world is a beautiful home for the Self, but temporary. This home can become peaceful and comfortable while the Self is here only if its temporariness and purpose are realized. Life is a bridge -- a bridge the Self has to use to cross over into the Supreme Reality, the Real Home. This will complete the long journey of Self-knowing through Creation.

Worldly structures are beautiful, and relevant to life, but they are not the true home of the Self. They are like an eggshell to mature the Self for hatching. The Self has to move on, fly out, and seek the Supreme Reality. The Self has to detach from this space it loves and is familiar with. A lot of energy is locked in maintaining these structures. This energy has to be freed for deeper experiences and merging with the Supreme Being. Besides, the Self has no choice. The egg becomes stale if the chick, once ready, does not hatch. We can see it in the world today. The Self has sufficiently evolved and is ripe for seeking the Supreme Reality but is not letting go its existing structures. This is causing disorder, degeneration, and unhappiness in the Self. Nothing can remain healthy in Creation if it is not freely flowing, constantly excelling, and answering the original purpose.

Enter the Supreme Reality, which is Your True Home while living here. This is the purpose of life. The Supreme Being is waiting for you to arrive.

All religions of the past used the word Home very meaningfully to convey information about the realm of Supreme Reality. To inspire the desire for this realm in the Self whose mind was childlike and innocent in those times, this eternal home was described as heaven, having supreme illumination, unimaginable beauty, unearthly pleasures, angels, no darkness ever, no misery and pain ...

There is no greater joy than arriving home after a long journey. You will be yourself, complete, at rest, and have peace.

19

True Living

*True living is living to know the Supreme Being,
to fall in love with the Supreme Being.
True living is a life on the path toward the
Supreme Being.
Finding the Supreme Reality is the quest for
which the Self is in Creation. Only a life lived
toward it is true.*

True living is entering the path toward experiencing the Supreme Being. The Self enters the path once the Truth is revealed to it and its original quest is awakened. Only a life on this path has peace and happiness.

The Self should live from love, faith, and reason. These are the three pillars of life in Creation. Base your understanding of them on the Supreme Truth. There is no higher living than there is when all three are present. It will purify the Self. It will free the Self. Every new Truth you come to know should be lived. It should work. Truth always works. It is never just a belief. It should increase your peace and happiness. This is the proof that the new Truth is higher, and in the right direction.

The Self has to become a true learner. Life has to be approached always with a question, not to verify a conclusion. This question should be of the Self. It should be asked personally. The Self has to remain open to the new, always.

The Self should seek guidance from those who know about the Truth from experience. This will give results, make the process easier, and develop humility in the Self, without which no progress can be made on the path toward the Supreme Being.

The mind, body, and senses are instruments of living. The Self is rooted into life through them. A life of balance heals them. They have to be purified. Abusing them for pleasure destroys them. They have to be prepared for experiencing the Supreme Reality.

Living should become an Attached-Detachment. It should be detached from the awareness that the individual Self and physical reality is a temporary state; and it should be attached by knowing that the Self is living for a purpose. Life has to be loved in order to arrive at the answer the Self seeks. This will give the best balance to the Self to live in a family and society, and remain a seeker of the Supreme Truth.

The Self has to constantly work on freeing the mind from the "I." The "I" has to be watched all the time. A little inattentiveness, and it will take over. The "I" does not exist in silence and attentiveness. The Self should live in one of the two states. Practice humility in life because the "I" does not survive in it.

Sharing what you have come to know with others is also a quality of true living. It deepens your Self-knowing. But share only what you have experienced, and only as much you have understood. Guidance from true experience is always helpful.

Reconnect with the Supreme Source. This will open the flow of spiritual energy, joy, peace, and guidance to the Self. Cut off from its Source, the Self has to fulfill its vital needs of energy and joy in unnatural and inefficient ways. Thoughts, power, sex, and food meet these needs. But these keep the Self anchored only to the material world, and its attention engaged on lower centers of consciousness. In this kind of existence, a human being is like an animal. Even an animal is better -- an animal is a lower form of life, but is connected with Nature for its needs, which keeps its living true and balanced. A Self ignorant of Reality is separated from its Source; it becomes dysfunctional, depleted, unhappy, fearful, and tense. To live toward the Supreme Reality, all areas of life (sleeping, thinking, reasoning, relating, working, eating, etc.) have to be purified and freed to become real before the Self can experience it.

Reviving Feeling, the core faculty of the Self, is the key thing. The five senses are the instruments of feeling on the physical level, and they have to be healed. The "I" centered Self has existed too long in its thoughts, disconnected from real life. The senses no longer perceive pure physical reality like a child. They have narrowed down and have become perverted. Feeling and senses have to be freed from a disinterested, ignorant, and conditioned mind. It is a rare human being today who uses all five senses fully. It is a rare human being today who can feel anything without a deep stimulation. After the five senses are revived, and become clear, the Self has to develop the five inner senses: Inner seeing, Inner Hearing, Inner Smelling, Inner Tasting, and Inner Touch. Both inner and outer feeling and unwavering attention are essential for experiencing the Supreme Being.

True living transforms the Self. The true Self becomes childlike, as well as awakened. It has the innocence, spontaneity, openness, playfulness, love and trust in life of a child; and the awakening to the Supreme Reality of a Mystic. Supreme Joy is natural in this state of True Living. Progress toward the Supreme Reality is effortless.

Since Prophets, Saints, and Mystics are your source for knowing about Supreme Reality as well your models for True Living, know a truth. Without it you would not see them in the true light and be able to draw right conclusions from their lives for your own life. Every being in Creation has to follow the same laws; there can be no exception, regardless of whether you are a Saint or a Sinner. Until you see this, there will be an unreal distance between you and these Great Beings. Do not exalt them to a spiritually exclusive class and worship them, for an eventual place in Heaven. This way you will not be able to see their real beauty and trueness. The Saints evolved the same way as every Self would have to. At one time, they had the same weaknesses as you. What you see and revere is a finished product -- an excellent finished product in Creation. They loved the Supreme Being more than anyone, endlessly worked harder than anyone, and ultimately purified the Self till it became crystal clear to receive Divine illumination. They did not stop there, and tested their Truth on the touchstone of life against ultimate challenges. To be a true seeker, you have to take responsibility for your own life and appreciate how hard they worked. If you have to take a leaf out of their book, it should be love, unwavering faith, strength, and hard work. Why belittle them by thinking they were granted this status without doing anything in Creation? They lived truly and fully, and that is how they became larger than life.

True Heaven is personal, and is the supreme quality of existence of the Self. In this very world, the Self can enter its heaven or hell depending upon its way of living, understanding, and choosing. Love the Supreme Being, and live from the Truth more and more. The Saints also travelled toward their Heaven on this path: LOVE AND TRUE LIVING.

Never forget that life is an invaluable opportunity!

Human life did not happen to us by chance. How would you feel if you knew how much you wanted to be here; if you knew you were one of the countless souls urging to live here -- if you knew about your immense urge for physical experience; if you knew your original urge could most deeply be realized only in this world? What if you knew that the bridge to ultimate bliss is physical experience of our ultimate Truth? You would hold this chance to live with both hands. From this very moment, you would put your entire soul into knowing who you are. You would begin deeply respecting every experience in every moment. You would become grateful to everything Creation gives to you. You would know how much intelligence and care Creation exercises to provide you with unique experiences. A limitless love would arise within you for yourself, your family, the entire world, the whole universe. Every breath we have, every grain of food we eat, every drop of water we drink, every loving hug we receive, the earth beneath our feet, the sky and stars above us, all play an unimaginable role to expand our consciousness.

There is no love for The Infinite that is greater than love for living. There is no faith in The Infinite greater than abandoning to life.

We do not do the smallest thing in our life without knowing its purpose. How can we live without knowing the purpose of such an immense thing as life? In everything, we first feel and decide our motive, and then begin. If we are unsure of our motive we become disinterested. We become indecisive. We cannot plan. We cannot organize. We cannot manage. We get no result. We become unhappy. We lose hope. We lose feeling. We become disconnected from life. Have we ever thought about what meaning life has for us? What meaning so many other things in our life have for us? We love life, so we have to ask these questions of ourselves.

From a grain of sand, a blade of grass, or a drop of water, to many distant stars, we have come to know something about the world. We think we will arrive at an ultimate knowing by dividing and microscopically looking into things in the infinitely vast physical Universe. We disregard the fact that this visible Universe is itself an infinitesimal speck in the unknowable vastness beyond. We think we will analyze data, theorize, and understand The Whole. And once we have ultimate knowing, we will have power over everything in Creation -- even life and death. But all we are growing is a very knowledgeable, confused, complicated, doubtful, disordered, unhappy, discontented, and restless mind. And its center we perceive as our "I." Our present self-identity is an illusion, and it is impermanent. Our experience is incomplete because it is relative, partial, and extremely limited. The new reveals itself every day but our Ultimate Truth remains elusive. Why? Because there is one domain we have never entered -- the search for our source and our true Self. It is in this realm that we will experience what we are actually seeking: spontaneous knowing, uncaused happiness, everlasting identity, and infinite living!!!

Life is Infinite. Your Self is Infinite. The purpose of Creation is Infinite. Absolute power cannot be possessed. You can become one with it. Happiness and Peace can be found. But the way is different. You have to know and experience The Supreme Reality in order to arrive at them. Even the first step on the path toward it will make you feel the true flavor of Reality.

Now it is your choice, whether to continue in the direction you are now living and suffer in turmoil, or change course toward your Self and its Reality.

Above all, love for the Supreme Being should become the be-all and end-all of life. Only a life lived in this seeking is true.

20

Bliss

Bliss is supreme joy felt during oneness with the Supreme Being. It is peace, happiness, contentment, awareness, and all what the Self has ever sought, together in one experience.

Bliss is the feeling when the Self experiences the Supreme Being. In this state, there is no Self -- only the Supreme Being is.

The first experiences of bliss are felt when the Self is falling in love with the Supreme Being. During this stage, the Self seeks everywhere for more knowledge about the Supreme Being. The Self reads many books. It seeks beings that have experienced the Supreme Being. The more the Self knows about the Supreme Being the deeper its bliss becomes.

As love for the Supreme Being takes complete hold of the Self, sweet nothings, passion, pining for just a glimpse, become the Self's whole life. The only wish of the Self now is to lose itself, in this love. It is prepared to give everything for a meeting, even prepared to die. In this stage of yearning, restlessness, impatience, and gasping like a fish out of water for an experience -- even the pain of separation itself is bliss.

As love further deepens, the Supreme Being pulls the Self into an embrace occasionally. This is an ecstasy that is earthshaking. It is like a million orgasms together. The mind and the body have never felt such ecstasy. After each union the intense feeling continues for days. The mind and the body have never felt such an infinite happiness. They remain ungrounded in material reality for a long time. It is like passing a very high voltage through the fragile wiring of the mind and the body. These fragile instruments gradually get conditioned to the bliss of deeper and deeper spiritual experiences.

Finally, love closes the gap between the Supreme Being and the Self, to complete oneness -- bliss becomes everlasting. Now oneness of the Supreme Being, Self, and Creation can be experienced in every moment of life. This is the realm of Supreme Living. The senses are now pure, the mind is true, and the Self's expression is constantly excelling.

The last and Supreme Bliss is in ultimate merging with the Supreme Being. This spontaneously happens when the Self has expressed its complete potential and beauty in Creation.

Every experience with the Supreme Being is endless bliss.

21

Path

Enter a love affair with the Supreme Being.

To enter a love affair with the Supreme Being, fall in love with the Supreme Being. To fall in love with the Supreme Being you have to know about the Supreme Being first. You already know a little, from expressions of the Supreme Being visible to you in the world. Here the beloved is unknown and is formless. You have to know more in order to fall in love. Here the beloved is Infinite and endless. You have to continue to fall in love all your life, deeper and deeper, as more beauty is revealed. Once you fall in love, you will want an experience of the beloved. It is natural. For that, live toward experiencing the Supreme Being. True living is such a life. Once you experience the Supreme Being your heart will yearn for more and deeper experiences of the beloved. Love more, until your love causes selflessness and, you experience selfless love. Once that happens, you will want eternal oneness with the beloved. Live for complete dissolution of the "I," and it will happen. I have followed this path and am still in love. My love affair will continue till I am in Creation.

In this book I have revealed enough from my experiences with Supreme Being for you to fall in love. I have also explained all the areas of the Self and life which are related to this love affair. If your time has come it will begin. If not, what the book has revealed about the Supreme Reality will prepare you for it. In any case the process has begun. I told you when you entered this book that you will not be the same again after reading it. You decide whether I was right or wrong.

Life should become a seeking, and an expression of love for the Supreme Being. Talking about the Supreme Being, singing the praises of the Supreme Being, knowing more about the Supreme Being, meditating on the Supreme Being, true living to prepare and beautify the Self for the Supreme Being -- all of these should keep this relationship of love active every moment. The Self should see the Supreme Being in everything in Creation, and love everything with the same feeling. Love for the Supreme Being should saturate every feeling, thought, and act. Every happening in life should be seen as an act of the Supreme Being, and loved from complete surrender. Even pain and misery should not be questioned in this love. You should feel that nothing the Beloved does can be wrong. The Supreme Being's presence should be prayed for in everything the Self does. There is no question that the Supreme Being will respond to such TOTAL LOVE.

The Supreme Being should become the only seeking in life. Only one path should be followed from total faith. Never question it. Never compare your path with other paths.

Love the Supreme Being more than yourself. Work on freeing the Self from the "I," its pride and fears. In order to do this, live from Love, Faith, and Reason. Free the Self from pride by practicing humility. Free the Self from attachments by becoming detached. Live a simple and balanced life. The love affair will keep on becoming more and more passionate as energies held in other loves and hates become free.

Catch the flame of love from a Master. Experience a Master for deepening the love. Know more about the Supreme Being from a Master. A Master is the ultimate lover. Masters are not guides or teachers. They just are what they are. Love for the Supreme Being is demonstrated spontaneously in their acts. See them express love for the Supreme Being all the time, while they eat, drink, drive, work, joke, fight, or whatever they do. Just being near them opens the heart to love for the Supreme Being. Once addicted to this love, the Self can love nothing else.

Listen to the voice of the heart. Use reason to become free of the mind. The blocks of self-image, illusions, past conditioning, and compulsive behavior will gradually dissolve. There is a touchstone to know whether it is the heart's voice or the mind's: following the heart's voice should make the Self feel freer and happier. Love will further deepen.

Completely surrender to the Supreme Being in love. Never think you have loved so much and the Supreme Being has not responded yet. Your focus should be on loving more and more. Many subtle attachments of the Self to its "I" will prevent surrender from becoming total. Always remember that the Supreme Being is equally yearning for your love. Just continue to love with the whole being -- The Supreme Being will respond; a meeting will happen!!!

Love, love, and only love is the way to the Supreme Being.

22

Mystic

WHO ARE THE MYSTICS?

Mystics are seekers of The Truth. Mystics are lovers of The Reality. They seek actual experience of the Supreme Being. Their passion and quest arise from love for The Infinite and desire to arrive at The Ultimate Reality. They live simple and balanced lives toward it. They are completely surrendered to the Supreme Being, Creation, and life.

All through history they have shown the way to others after experiencing their own Truth. They de-mystify The Truth, live and demonstrate it, and put people on the path so that they can experience it for themselves. Miracles happen around them spontaneously. They do not perform miracles for displaying metaphysical powers or for material benefit. They are not the Psychics who merely have the ability to know and materialize a few deeper levels of Reality.

Mystics respect everything. They deny nothing. Their paths toward Reality go through a balanced blend of scientific exploration, processes of true religion, and love for the Supreme Being, Creation, and life.

Experience a true Mystic if you are in a quest to seek and experience The Supreme Truth.

23

Last Page

Unawakened living has driven the Self and Earth into a situation where healing is urgently required. The Self needs healing, families need healing, communities need healing, organizations need healing, beliefs need healing, love needs healing, faith needs healing, the planet needs healing .... Begin now.

What can you give to others when you continue to cheat your own Self? Be alone with your Self for a few moments. You will hear its deep cry for true living. Plundering others and the environment is wrong. Fear of God, Divine punishment, Morality, and Guilt scare every Self and keep it in check. But plundering your own Self for skin deep, fleeting, just sensual pleasures is no less wrong. The punishment of Creation for this is even more severe. The way out from false living is not easy. Modern living has lost all balance and naturalness and has gone to excess. Nemesis should never be overprovoked. Otherwise Creation would be left with no option but purging of ignorant attitudes and erasing structures created by vain pride. Human history shows this cycle of peaking of ignorant and unnatural living and vast cleansing. Great civilizations in the past fell and have gone into oblivion because human beings challenged or ignored The Supreme Truth. This has happened many times. Human pride, greed, and ignorance caused these disasters. Immense knowledge and achievement has been lost repeatedly because lessons were never learnt. Earth is at a critical point in human evolution again -- the human mind has become vastly expanded and science is very advanced. Human beings have begun to challenge and ignore the Supreme Truth again. Whether our civilization will suffer the same fate again or will be exalted to higher dimensions of consciousness will depend upon what direction the human mind will take from here during the coming time -- the one going toward disaster or the one going toward awakening.

We have evolved a very knowledgeable and complicated mind. It grows larger every day. But The Ultimate Truth remains as out of its grasp as ever. Our present impermanent and unstable identity is its center. We call it our "I." The mind, which by its very nature is relative, fragmented, insecure, fearful, conflicting, lonely, doubtful, discontented, greedy, and restless -- we think this mind will become our bridge to Reality. Some of us think the process of science will arrive at an ultimate knowing. So we continue to divide, microscopically look at things, analyze data, understand a few new things, and feel encouraged that we are deciphering The Secret of Life. And very soon we will have the final answer and power over life and death. Then some new disease strikes, and we panic and run helter-skelter for answers. Others think unquestioning faith in a Religion that is just beliefs is the answer. So heaven and facts of life are seen as two different Realities. The hope is that we will be pardoned and rescued at the end and given the Reality we desire and cannot have here.

SEEK THE SUPREME BEING. EXPERIENCE THE SUPREME REALITY. KNOW THE TRUTH.

Do not hesitate. Do not feel embarrassed. Nothing about the Supreme Being is irrational. If there is anything irrational in this world it is the limited basis a human mind uses for belief or disbelief. Unfortunately, most knowing about the Supreme Being and Reality is just a product of thought and imagination, and therefore fragmentary. The mind is very powerful. It can reason in any direction and can play tricks, even of enlightenment, with you. You can continue to believe any Reality is true and ultimate and that you have arrived. If it is not a fact, the peril is yours.

A clue about what powerful transformation happens within the Self after experiencing the Supreme Being can be picked by truly exploring the lives of Saints, Prophets, and Mystics of the past. They all lived here to demonstrate a life beyond awakening. But an open mind is a prerequisite; otherwise your mind will just see what it wants to see.
Whatever your existing belief is about The Truth -- apply it in real life. Life is the touchstone. It should give you peace and happiness. If it does not, then seek a new Truth.

CPSIA information can be obtained at www.ICGtesting.com
Printed in the USA
BVOW022215110911

270977BV00001B/202/P